Irish Earth Folk

Irish Earth Folk

By DIARMUID MAC MANUS

Illustrated

THE DEVIN-ADAIR COMPANY · NEW YORK · 1959

Canadian agent: Thomas Nelson & Sons, Ltd., Toronto

Library of Congress catalog card number: 59–13563

Manufactured in the United States of America

Designed by Lewis F. White

In memory
of my loved
and revered friend
the late WILLIAM BUTLER YEATS

Preface

I have been pleasantly surprised at the number of people I have met in recent years who take an intelligent interest in the ancient and continuing spirit life of the countryside.

Silly people who talk glibly of "fairies at the bottom of the garden" have provided invaluable ammunition for the equally silly know-it-alls who jeer and gibe at the whole thing. So I have endeavored to pull the subject out of the morass of nonsense and counternonsense and to get it into the realm of logic, where it can be examined coolly and sympathetically. To do so I have first outlined the traditional background of these curious things and have then given accounts of various happenings which will be sufficient, I hope, to enable readers to start thinking things out for themselves.

In regard to these accounts, I have adhered strictly to certain principles, except in a few instances. In the few cases where I have not, I have made it abundantly clear. The principles are these. In the first place, a central character in each incident is still alive. Secondly, he is reliable, and thirdly, he is prepared to stand over it firmly. And in all cases the incidents are well authenticated and can be verified by anyone. In no case have I gone more than five miles out of my way to get a story. Except in a few instances, those telling the stories have been personal friends of mine for years.

I also want to make it clear that I am no folklorist and do not attempt to write as one. I am merely a historian, recording as accurately as I can various happenings of recent times. Most Irish fairy tales published in the past have been traditional ones, in as much as the storyteller is repeating what he has heard from others who have themselves only heard it. So all those tales are just nursery entertainments and are without any relation to everyday life. Yet Douglas Hyde and William Butler Yeats, who both recorded much, were fully aware of the "everyday" aspect of fairy lore and had great respect for it.

Dr. Hyde, a very prominent collector of traditional Irish tales and poems and later first president of Ireland, was an old family friend. He and my aunt, Lottie Mac Manus, were closely associated in many activities, especially in the fields of language and folk life. I used to learn much from him in the early 1920s when I saw him most often. I knew and revered that charming poet, painter, and mystic AE (George Russell) too and was intimate with Yeats in his later years. I am well aware how affectionately and seriously these great and cultured minds regarded the spirit life of rural Ireland. Though it has always fascinated me, I feel sure I would never have written this book but for their good influence. In doing so I wish only to persuade other reasonable people to treat it also with interest and sympathy.

I have avoided witchcraft like wildfire, for it is much

too dangerous to handle. At this moment I could fill three chapters with recent stories of it, but every story would bristle with libel actions as a hedgehog does with spines.

I have used noms-de-plume in those few cases where I have not received specific permission to use real names. I have written all these stories with entire sincerity, and I am satisfied that they have been given to me in full sincerity. I feel sure they will be read with equal sincerity.

D. Mac Manus

Dublin, 1959

Contents

Preface   vii

I   The Middle Kingdom   3

II   The Fairy Folk   20

III   Fairy Trees   45

IV   The Pooka   61

V   Magic Cures   77

VI   Pranks and Mischief   99

VII   Fairy Ground and Paths   123

VIII   The Stray Sod   144

IX   Hostile Spirits and Hurtful Spells   158

X   Biddy Early   176

Illustrations

(*between pages 114 and 115*)

The Killeaden thorn tree

A fairy fort

The famous fairy fort of Lis Ard

A fairy oak on Lis Ard

The demon thorn tree

Paddy Baine's house, with corner removed

The river Gweestion, where the "stray sod" was effective

The fairy trilogy of oak, ash, and thorn

The road of the three dark figures

The Big House, where Biddy Cosgary lived

Martin Groak and Mac Manus family members

Irish Earth Folk

CHAPTER I

The Middle Kingdom

In Tir-ha'n-Og,
In Tir-ha'n-Og,
The Blackbird lilts, the Robin chirps, the Linnet wearies never,
They pipe to dancing feet of Sidhe and thus shall pipe for ever.
Ethna Carbery

The claims of human beings that they have seen and have made physical contact with spiritual beings are universal and eternal. The human community, ancient or modern, highly civilized or savage, that has no knowledge of, or belief in, spiritual beings of some kind has yet to be found. Even the iron tyranny of communism has utterly failed to abolish contact with spirit life.

Though the accounts of these beings differ widely, from race to race and from time to time, the differences are largely superficial, and deep and basic unities remain.

3

But the differences are reasonable and natural, for races differ in characteristics and powers. Some races are physically tall and broad-shouldered, with fair hair and wide faces, or high cheek bones and flat noses. Others are dark and squat or slim and sharp-faced. Also their mental powers differ, some being quick-witted and others slow, some quick-tempered, others placid. And in exactly the same way their psychic powers differ: the Finns, Swedes, and Magyars in Europe, for example, are historically known for their highly developed occult powers, while the Saxons, Dutch, and Wends are far behind. The Celts are well above the European average while the English are below it, although in the Celtic pockets of England, such as Devon and Cornwall, the fairy tradition has been kept alive. The same is found in Brittany and Southwest France.

It is a commonplace to call primitive peoples "children of nature" and to apply the same term to youngsters unspoilt by conventions or city living. Are we not all born clear-sighted, and is it not our artificial surroundings and upbringing which destroy this ability? Children are much better able to make psychic contacts than grown-ups are, for their natural powers have not yet been atrophied by artificiality. In the same way, on the purely physical side a city dweller cannot hear nor see nor smell with the keenness of a jungle tracker who has never left nature nor been unfaithful to it in any way but has kept his powers in constant use. From the very beginning until modern times the vast majority of the human race has been steeped in the country and has lived close to nature in a way that is very difficult for people in this mechanized age to appreciate.

In olden days the strength and vitality of a race lay in its healthy and virile country communities, living their self-sufficient lives according to nature's plan, for they were an integral part of it. Their lives were interwoven with the wonders of the eternal seasons, of birth and of death, of fertility and growth. They knew and loved, even if inarticulately, the beauty which God has evolved by His divine laws of nature, and the spiritual outlook was never absent from them.

Today the country is merely the adjunct of the cities, and in these the balance of power entirely lies; the dwindling rural districts have been degraded into a mere food factory to supply the teeming millions of the towns. The more universally town rule and factory regulations are brought into the country, the more materialistic the country must become and the more divorced from the beauty and from the spirits of nature.

Today, for instance, the planting of trees is not done as it used to be, when oak and beech and thorn were set with pride and hope for the beauty they would provide for another generation a hundred years on and more. Quick-growing soft woods and firs are now put down, that they may bring in material gain within a lifetime. And as materialism comes in, in many lands, so the old contacts with the spirit world of nature go out. Even in Ireland the materialists in the towns, with their newly acquired superficial education without wisdom, are attacking vigorously. But contacts with the spirit world have not yet vanished from Ireland and please God they never will, and this book is the proof that they are still here.

Do not let anyone imagine that I have had to travel far and wide, painstakingly collecting stories here and there as if plucking rare and precious flowers. Not in the least; for the stories have come to me without strenuous searching on my part; indeed, I have had to pick and choose from

a large number. Many of these tales I have known and
lived with for years; others, which are more recent, I have
come across without special effort and in the course of my
daily life. On no occasion have I gone as far afield as five
miles to hear a story.

In Ireland the world of the Shee (*Sidhe*), that is, of
the fairies and of all those spirits which are elemental and
have never been human, was called the Middle Kingdom,
a satisfactory and expressive term. In ancient times, and
almost up to this very age, this world of "faerie" has been
as much an accepted reality to the country people as has
the normal material world around them. But today, though
belief still remains widespread, the old knowledge of the
organization, of the ordered hierarchy, of the classes and
castes that compose the spirit world has almost disappeared. In fact, quite often ghosts, which properly are departed human spirits, are roughly and tactlessly lumped
together with all the grades of leprechauns, cluricauns,
pookas, seal folk, merrows, demons, and the rest, as if all
were the same.

How do the ancient stories of gods and heroes, of men
and spirits, with their accurate grading in the spirit world,
come about? They are handed down by tradition. All traditional tales are the repetition of past human experiences.
Some of those which survive and which are more in con-
sonance with the material world around us are looked upon
as the background of history. Others, more difficult to fit
into the normal way of life, are too often put aside as being
the result of imagination or invention. Some stories of both
kinds may well be tales of olden heroes whose deeds, great
at the time, have been made greater still as the years have
passed. In the course of time the great gods of Celtic

mythology have probably become inextricably mixed with
the old heroes, now raised to the position of demigods.

As with every race and through every generation since
speech began, so it has been with the Irish: the family
always has been the center of the verbal recording of history. When the day's work has been done and the family
—the tribal family, once much larger than ours of today
and including uncles and aunts and cousins—has gathered
round the fire, and when hunger has been satisfied and the
shadows have lengthened, an elder, or perhaps a traveling
bard, begins to talk and to recount old stories. The children listen with rapt attention, drinking them in word for
word, and in due course pass them on to their own children in turn.

Under that old, elaborate Celtic organization the more
heroic tales would quickly be taken up by the professional
bards, who would develop them artistically along highly
conventional lines, often expanding them to enormous
lengths. It was during this process that exaggeration usually took place. Professor Delargy, Director of the Irish
Folklore Commission, heard of a wandering beggarman—
of modern times—in West Kerry who took seven nights to
repeat one tale. One of the commission's staff recorded a
tale of 34,000 words from a Connemara storyteller who
knew at least 350 tales, long and short. There must have
been even greater feats of that kind in ancient days, when
illiteracy was general and memory in constant use.

But the bards specialized only in the heroic sagas, the
tales of gods and heroes, for these were of wide interest
and general concern, enthralling their listeners whenever
they were told. Tales of domestic life or of encounters with
the earth folk were useless to the bards, for such stories
were commonplaces; encounters were had continually by

the ordinary people round about. With few exceptions, these common stories were left to the old people who had no need to hark back in time but who told of what they knew themselves or what their parents knew. The same happenings are going on today, and it is of them that I have gathered a few stories here.

Except perhaps during the first generation, it is difficult for the storyteller to change or embroider stories of heroic kind, for too many others know them and are instantly ready to put an error right. Professor Kenneth Jackson, of Edinburgh University and President of the Scottish Anthropological and Folklore Society, emphasizes this safeguard and I have often heard it in operation myself. This is one of the great causes of the remarkable accuracy, now generally acknowledged by scholars, of important traditional stories.

William Butler Yeats, writing in 1893 in the introduction to his *Irish Fairy and Folk Tales,* says: "Stories have been handed down with such accuracy that the long tale of Deirdre was, in the earlier decades of this century, told almost word for word as in the very ancient ms. in the Royal Dublin Society. In one case only it varied, and then the ms. was obviously wrong—a passage had been forgotten by the copyist. But this accuracy is rather in the folk and bardic tales than in the fairy legends, for these vary widely."

On the same theme Professor Jackson has said: "The story of Deirdre as collected in Barra by Carmichael and the version of the life of Chulainn which he got in South Uist, are in some respects extraordinarily close to the manuscript tales which can be traced back in Ireland to the ninth century in written form and no one knows how much further in oral." Professor Delargy also tells us of a

Kerry shanachie, or storyteller, who had heard a large
part of the printed edition of Diarmuid and Grainne read
in his youth; fifty years later the professor took it down
from him and found that it agreed almost word for word
with the original printed text.

Now, in regard to those tales which are clearly historical, though often with wonders and magic thrown in
to improve them, we can see in our own time just how they
arose and started upon their period of growth. We have
them in the "Come-all-ye's" sung in every town and village of the land and at every cottage dance during and
since that period of unrest now euphemistically called "the
troubles." In these songs the deeds of local as well as of
national heroes were extolled, and the descriptions of their
prowess lost nothing in the repetition. But as the years
pass and other events upsurge between the then and the
now, the call for them decreases. The original singers and
tellers are dead, and those who today pass on these stirring
tales know not those brave and wild days, so they repeat
by rote what they have learned by ear. Thus, already these
things have passed into the realm of verbal history, the
value of which must depend upon the accuracy which they
maintained during the first hectic years.

When, in recent times, there has been embroidery, it
has been within reason. It is extremely rare—I, personally,
have heard only three instances—for any occult or magic
flavor to enter into those tales. But in ancient times, when
the spirit and the material worlds were so closely inter-
mixed in the minds of men, it was a very different matter.
It was easy to attach wonders, when they happened to be
lacking, to these old heroes. When wonders enough had
been added, the next step was simple: the heroes would
become raised to the status of demigods and would take

their permanent places in the higher pagan hierarchy. As this transformation took place, their human acts tended also to be transfigured into even greater magic and breathtaking wonders, and such tales must later be looked upon as apocryphal in a high degree, though always with a background of truth and reality. The unraveling of these tangled skeins is the fascinating duty of the prehistory historian.

The raising of humans to high place in the heavenly world is ancient and universal. The pagan Romans raised their emperors to the position of gods.

The fact that the same stories sometimes are to be found in many lands does not necessarily mean that they are all mere repetitions of one original incident which has become grossly exaggerated. For instance, the same tales may be found in ancient Greece, in India, and in other countries, but they all can have their origins in the various localities independently, in satisfaction of some universal need.

Admittedly some of these tales are the same ancient story, rehashed to fit into a local situation, and so are genuinely allegories. I merely suggest that there are exceptions to this reading of them, especially where the tale is heroic rather than Olympian. As a case in point, I know an officer in England who ran off with the lovely young wife of his commanding officer. Whatever its ethics, it was an act of great daring, but it was far from being recognized as such by the authorities, and my acquaintance had to send in his papers and leave the service without delay. Taking the milder manners of modern times into consideration, this may be looked upon as much the same dénouement as in the cases of Diarmuid and Grainne and of Paris and Helen.

Yet it would be difficult to maintain the thesis that the modern abduction never took place but is only an invented modern variation of the original Trojan tale.

Besides these historical tales, there are the quite different Celtic religious tales, the earlier ones of which concern the great pagan gods and goddesses and their dealings with men and with each other. Later these often merge almost imperceptibly into the tales of the early saints and of their works and wonders. These pagan gods, the great Shee of the Celts, require care in classification for, of right, they should each personify some spiritual ideal or an aspect of the infinite All-Being behind all that exists.

In still a different class are the tales of common men and women in their relations with one another, of the eternal struggles between the stupid and the clever, the wicked and the good, or the old and the young; all these throw light upon the manners and customs of past times and can be much more readily taken at their face value. Hearing them, one sees clearly how delightfully consistent is basic human nature throughout the world in every race and clime, in every age and time.

Last of all there are the stories of human encounters with the small spirits, the "wee folk" of Ulster, the "little people" of the South, the "Shee-og" of Gaeldom, and with all the other minor elementals that are on much the same earth level. It is with these encounters, occurring within recent times, that we are concerned in this book. For we are not here interested in the great spirits, except occasionally and then only very indirectly, but in those lesser beings which our country people—and not only peasants, by any means—have seen and still claim to see. These spirits might be called the plebeians of the Middle King-

dom. They are the lower grades of that august and interesting society, and even they range up and down in the
social scale quite widely.

Before proceeding further it is well that we get our
definitions clear, especially as to what we mean by "fairy."
Skeat's *Etymological Dictionary* tells us that in olden times
it meant not a being at all but "a spell by a fay," and that
"fay" comes from the Latin goddess of Fate. However, for
centuries "fairy" has meant a spirit of some kind, but of
what particular kind we must now determine. Difficulty
arises chiefly through the widespread, inexact use of the
expression "fairy folk" to mean all occult beings or, certainly, all minor earth folk. But this common use of "fairy"
as a generic term, though very convenient, is inaccurate
and unjustified.

The best traditional test of the fairy nature lies in the
belief, universally accepted throughout Europe from ancient classical times up to today, that humans and fairies
can intermarry and interbreed, begetting children by each
other, and can exchange children; each can live successfully in the other's world. The Celtic stories of fairy women
marrying men and begetting and rearing children by them,
and of men and women passing their lives among "the
people of the mounds" are innumerable. Alasdair Mac-
Gregor in his fascinating book on Scots folklore, *The
Peat-Fire Flame,* gives many accounts of seal women
discarding their fish-tail garment and coming ashore to
marry a human, begetting children and eventually being
drawn back to the sea after many years by intense nostal-
gic longing, generally brought about by unexpectedly coming across the old fish dress. These tales are widespread
throughout all the Hebrides and along the northern and
western coasts of Ireland. Tales of the kidnaping of human

children or of depositing changelings in the cradle are
common everywhere too.

We must, then, include as fairies the seal folk, leprechauns, cluricauns, and banshees, and in England and
Scotland the pixies, brownies, and glaistigs. Gnomes,
dwarfs, and pookas may have a claim for recognition, but
I propose to exclude them arbitrarily for the convenience
of my own classification, even at the risk of hurting their
feelings.

The fairies most frequently referred to in medieval
times and up to the eighteenth century throughout Europe
were those living inside hills, where they were reputed
to have great halls and all the good things that humans
had, and they were of fine physique. This is quite in con-
sonance with the Irish Shee, for that Gaelic name really
means "the people who live in a mound." To be more pre-
cise, they were the *Sluagh Sidhe*, the hosts, or peoples, of
the mounds, for *Sidhe* seems merely to be the genitive of
Siodh, a mound or small hill. This is borne out when we
find them called in English "the people of the hills." It
is also very significant that in a part of Donegal they are
called *Sluagh Beatha*, the hosts of life, to my mind suggesting strongly that they were considered to be not those
dead and buried in barrows but vital and eternally living
people. This word "mound" has been taken to mean a barrow or tumulus, and it has been inferred that the Shee were
the ghosts of, or merely a living tradition of, past peoples
who buried their dead in these barrows. In spite of the
emphasis put on this interpretation by many folklorists, it
can be nothing more than an assumption and, I think, a
mistaken one, for the only active evidence that I know of
points in another direction. Such evidence is without exception consistent; in every trial of witches in which fairies

were mentioned as living in the earth, it was invariably in
a small natural hill that they dwelt and *not* in a barrow.
These fairies, then, were not thought, by those who had
known them, to be ghosts from tumuli, nor ancient human
races still alive.

I have never heard nor read—except in admitted fiction
—of any spirit which was associated with a human burial
ground that was not either a ghost, that is, the wraith of
a departed human, or an unpleasant elemental. By elemental I mean an earth spirit that is not a fairy in the
wider sense I have defined. In spite of the derivation of
the word "Shee" (*Sidhe*), the Great Ones of Irish paganism lived in high places—on mountaintops or in the very
air itself. They were earth free, unlike those minor spirits
we now call fairies, who are definitely earthbound, in common with all other earth folk.

Today, the word "fairy" has come to be associated with
everything that is unreal and childish. Shakespeare was
probably one of the first to draw attention to small sprites,
giving them great names and an importance that no tradition has justified. From this arose the nursery fairy stories
of the nineteenth century, and now we have the colorful
phantasies of Walt Disney and his confrères, flitting with
gay and vivid insouciance across the cinema screen.

By all these steps the word "fairy" has shifted away
completely from its medieval concept of a powerful spirit
in human form which should be treated with respect, if not
with a little fear, and has now become attached to dainty
little winged figures flitting like butterflies from flower to
flower or doing ballet dances with a starlit wand. The traditional fairies, though rarely dainty, are sometimes lovely;
but far more often, when small beings are reported to have
been seen, they are described as elflike.

According to accounts, the earth elementals cover a very wide range, from the awful and inhuman horrors of loathsome aspect and evil design, upwards through those beings which are impish and naughty, to the charming and merry, the lovely and sad and wistful; the higher ones being mostly of the fairy kind. The very small beings, only a few inches high, seem to be of the elf and imp type and are usually friendly as well as mischievous. The acts of these varied beings are closely associated with their nature and constantly impinge upon the daily lives of humans. These acts are none the less effective even if their spirit perpetrators do not appear. From all the accounts, it becomes clear that a consistent pattern of acts appears, by which the various beings and phenomena can be classified. When this is done, one sees with relief that no new or revolutionary evidence has come to light but that it all fits in comfortably with ancient tradition and is, therefore, all the more understandable.

Unlike the attitude of olden times, the viewpoint of today, on the rather rare occasions when a countryman stops to think it out, has a firm Christian basis. It seems now to be generally held that all these beings are angels who have fallen from heaven, but that very few of them have fallen so far as to be wholly evil. Those who have fallen utterly must show themselves looking as evil as they are, a fact which accounts for the horrible sights which are sometimes seen. These beings are poised between heaven and hell and are bound to the earth while humans occupy it. The better ones, the fairy folk, amuse themselves to keep their minds busy, and they copy the activities of men as much as possible, for they envy them. Through all their gaiety, their fun, and their activities there runs an inescapable vein of sadness, for they have lost heaven, while we can attain it, and they do not see any door leading back to it, as Christians have the door of their religion before them.

James Stephens, in *The Crock of Gold,* classifies many of these beings with admirable clarity and on the old pagan lines. He enumerates them all, however, both high and low, as if all were members of one undivided family, and he omits the tougher and more hostile ones. Of course, while the difference between the great ones of the Shee and the little earth-loving cluricauns and leprechauns is indescribably great, it is not possible to find a satisfactory dividing line anywhere, as the various types so gradually and imperceptibly merge into one another.

The most detailed information concerning the fairies, as apart from the rest of the earth folk, and in many ways concerning the demon world, too, comes from the sixteenth and seventeenth centuries, for they were the times of the great witch persecutions. Fairies, just as much as demons, were closely associated with the witches, especially in Scotland, France, and Sweden. A great deal of this information is juridical, detailed, and well annotated. In all cases, fairies are described as powerful beings living in highly organized communities and under a local king and queen. They are usually of human size or slightly larger and are fine looking, the men handsome, the women lovely, and all dignified.

In the first of her four famous confessions, dated April 13, 1662, the lovely young red-haired Scottish witch, Isobel Gowdie, a well-educated woman of good family, says: "I was in the Downie Hills and got meat there, more than I could eat. The Queen of Faerie is bravely clothed in white linen and in white and brown clothes; and the King of Faerie is a brave man, well-favoured and broad faced. There were elf bulls bellowing and squealing up and down there and affrighted me."

In the trial of Joan of Arc, fairies were discussed on all sides as being of human size. A leading biographer of Joan's says, "As for the fairies, the people of Domrémy set great store by them, for they had powers over the destinies of men."

In 1597 at Aberdeen, Isobel Strathaquin's daughter was quoted at her trial for witchcraft thus: ". . . that what skill so ever she has, she had it of her mother; and her mother learnt it of an elf-man who lay with her." In the same year Andrew Man, at his trial for the same offense, referred to the "Queen of Elfland." A few years later, in Orkney, Janet Drever was convicted of fostering a baby to the fairy folk in a local hill, whom she called "our good neighbours" and with whom she confessed to having had "carnal conversation" for over twenty years. Again, in 1664, Jonet Morrison was "accused" of healing with herbs a certain "Macfersone's daughter who had been blasted by the fairies with a very unnatural disease."

And so the tale goes on all over Europe. These few examples are typical of evidence given and accepted everywhere regarding the kind of being the fairy folk were considered to be in those days. Before that, right back to the days of classical paganism, they were very similar, though less well organized and not so concentrated in communities. For instance, all the nymphs, such as the lovely naiads, oreads, and nereids, were of human size and form, while the tales of their romantic and highly successful love affairs with humans were frequent. Fauns and satyrs, in spite of their usually, but by no means always, appearing with the lower limbs of a goat, were much the same. But these full-sized, vigorous fairies of the witch trials we see busy

at many of the same country crafts and employments that
men were occupied with, and they are utterly different
from the dainty wee butterfly sprites of Conan Doyle and
the writers of conventional "fairy tales." Any small spirits
that were mentioned in those days were of quite another
kind and were as often as not the "familiars" of the witches.
A familiar was supposed to be a wicked spirit which took
on an animal or even insect form and lived with a witch
so as to assist her in her hurtful activities against her neighbors.

Clearly many of these "spirits" were no more than the
pets of poor, lonely old women who, with no humans to
love, poured out their frustrated emotions upon living
things. The old lady who called her black cat "Sathan"
was asking for trouble, though such homely names as
Greedy Guts, Grissel, Robyn, Tyffin, Titty, and Pygine
seem redolent of harmlessness. None the less, other minor
spirits fit in fully with accepted tradition, for small household spirit retainers were ancient knowledge even when
the Lares and Penates of the Romans were at their height.
And what difference is there between these and the
brownies of Scotland and the cluricauns of Ireland today?
But in the rigid Christian times of the sixteenth and seventeenth centuries all these imps were classified by priest
and parson as demons let out from hell for our destruction.

The fairies known and seen in Ireland today keep cor-
rectly to tradition and have any height from that of a child
of six or seven to that of an unusually tall, fully grown man
or woman. I have heard only one tale claiming to be genuine that described little men of about one foot high, and
there is such conflict of evidence between the two boys
present that I cannot make use of it. So there appears still
to be the full rota of complementary spirits large and

small, all well able to interest us and even to annoy and
pester us.

William Butler Yeats, in his delightful *Celtic Twilight*,
tells us of "Paddy Flynn, a little bright-eyed old man who
lived in a leaky and one-roomed cabin in the village of
Ballisodare, which is, he was wont to say, 'the most gentle'
—whereby he meant faery—'place in the whole of County
Sligo.'" One day Yeats asked the old man if he had ever
seen the fairies and got the instant reply, "Am I not annoyed with them?" Later he mentions another woman who
did not believe either in hell or in ghosts but who added
confidentially, "But there are faeries and little leprechauns
and water-horses and fallen angels." Yeats concludes that
"no matter what one doubts, one never doubts the faeries,"
for, as a man said to him, "they stand to reason."

So let us see what these fairies and their activities are
today and whether they still "annoy" us, as old Paddy
Flynn so succinctly put it; and if so, in what way do they
do it. Above all, let us read of these doings with a friendly
eye.

CHAPTER II

The Fairy Folk

Up the airy mountain
  Down the rushy glen,
We daren't go a-hunting
For fear of little men.
    William Allingham

Ireland is a land where the quiet reality of the fairies is still accepted as a matter of everyday truth, in spite of the impact of the superficialities and robotisms of today's mechanical inventions. Of course, like other people the Irish are suffering from the artificial inanities of so much of the radio and of films, as well as from rushing, strident cars on our deepest country roads and nature-outraging tractors tearing up our fields. Our young people suffer from "practical" education which turns out standardized semi-educated minds—just as Ford's factories turn out cars.

But all the same, as long as countrymen dig in the fields and bogs in the gentle summer evenings and stroll home "betwixt the two lights," as they say, and in stumbling darkness go round the outhouses to see that the animals are safe and warm when the winter storms roar through the trees overhead, and as long as the girls milk the cows and with clever hands coax the last drops from the udder and tend the glowing turf fires on the open hearths, so long will they be close to the powers that live and pulsate in nature; and in this country those powers are, above all, the Shee, or, as the English call them, the fairies.

Our townies, alas, have already become slick and cynical and apart from mystic things; but the Irish country people, who are the true Irish, still have these powers of the spirit—though they are desperately shy of strangers or of any who might scoff and so they keep these things among themselves as closely as if they were not. And their ancient habit of friendly courtesy that bids them make their answer please rather than be overaccurate is still another bar upon their gate of reticence.

But if you are bred in the understanding of them or they can learn to trust you, then things of absorbing interest will come to light—with expressive words and well-rounded phrases dropping before you with a simplicity that gives a sense of trust and satisfies logic as well as heart.

Though I have all my life heard many stories and more half stories and dark references from the people at home, one of my chief aids has been the local schoolmaster. He and I were boys together in the country, and he is now the repository of much of the folklore of the district. With all his university degrees and wide learning, with his family of "modern" children now going out into the world

on their own, and with his social life in the little town, he
is, all the same, a believer in these occult things as a true
countryman should be—but, unlike most of them, he can
admit it openly. I was about to say he is a believer in spite
of his wisdom but checked myself in time, feeling that it
is *because* of this very wisdom.

And, more surprisingly, other firsthand stories have
come to me from city people whose background is deep
country and who have not forgotten it even after the
course of years.

To begin our fairy pilgrimage, let us first hear tales of
the fairy folk themselves—the "gentle people," as Yeats
and his friends often called them, for that is a Sligo tradition and for all I know may well be more widespread.
We hear of fairy trees and fairy forts and see them everyday in the Irish countryside, but what of the fairies themselves, the mysterious people who use them and so give
their name to them? From all I have ever heard of our
Irish fairies, and that is a great deal, they are truly "gentle
people" if they are not crossed, but beware of them indeed
if you deeply offend them. They are essentially country
beings, and they clearly love wild nature and are deeply
aware of its beauty and spiritual meaning as God's crea-
tion. They love the country people who fit into that crea-
tion so well and truly and from whom they often levy a
light and friendly tribute of milk or butter, honey or bread,
and suchlike produce of the earth, though they are sad at
man's destructive side and angry at his spreading icono-
clasm. They dance and sing and feast and love and in
many ways have the joys that mankind has, but a deep
sadness is supposed to run like a misty woof through the
warp of all their fun. In some things they know more than
any human can, but not in all things; indeed some of the

lower earth folk—though not the true fairies, the gentle
people—can be low and stupid in their minds as well. But
it is not safe to be too dogmatic about these people when
we know so little.

Our chief source of information is, and always must be,
country tradition; and after all, what is tradition but the
accumulated personal experiences of human beings which
have been handed down by the fireside from father to son
and from mother to daughter through generations past?
This tradition is a living thing, for it continues all the time,
and everyday some quota is added to it somewhere. Let
these fresh additions be given the full and serious deference which they deserve. In common with most country
people I have had contact with this living tradition, for I
have at one time or another personally met reliable men
and women who have assured me that they have themselves seen these "people" and they have described their
experiences to me in full. Most of them are living today, as
far as the stories in this book are concerned, and they can
be questioned at any time. In the cases where this is not
so, I have made it clear. These "seeings" are fairly rare but
they are, all the same, continually taking place, probably
even as I write this.

Here are some of the stories.

THE THORNHILL FAIRY

The first case was told to me by Colonel Henry Jordan. He is no longer alive, but the little girl in the story is
today happily married and flourishing. Colonel Jordan belonged to one of the oldest Norman families in Connacht,
and he lived in the ancient family home some five miles
distant from us. He was of my father's generation, though

younger, and our two families were close friends. The incident I now relate occurred some forty years ago, and
the old colonel told it to me in detail several times.

At the time it took place his youngest child, a daughter,
was about six or seven years old and his two other daugh-
ters were approaching, or just in, their teens. His English
wife had not been well and her niece, a charming girl of
eighteen called Nora, had come over from England to
help her with the young family. She had been there for
some time when, as she was dressing for dinner one evening and the little girl, who slept in her room, was watching her progress with great interest as she lay in her cot,
the first incident occurred.

Nora had placed the lamp on the dressing table before
the shuttered window and was peering into the glass as
she put the finishing touches to her hair, when the little
girl suddenly piped out, "Nora, Nora, there is a man in the
room. What is he doing here?"

At that, Nora turned round quickly to find herself face
to face with a little man about four feet high. He was
standing near the girl's cot and about nine or ten feet
from Nora—and he was as real and solid as anyone could
be. She stared at him in silent astonishment, and he returned her gaze with an expression of mild and aloof interest. But the next moment he had vanished before her
eyes and the room was as it had been.

It could be no trick of her imagination, for there was
the little girl sitting up in her cot and proclaiming that the
man had gone, just as if it were all quite natural and
proper. The child did not seem to be in the least perturbed
by the apparition or to think it particularly remarkable,
and Nora, to her own surprise, felt in no way nervous or
upset. One would have expected that, by its sheer uncan-

niness, the affair would have alarmed her, but the mild little man was clearly the soul of harmlessness.

Nora had made a very good inspection of him in the short time they had faced each other, and she could afterwards describe him clearly. Small though he was, he was perfectly proportioned, and he wore what were the traditional clothes of the country a century or more before. He had a green, brimless, "flowerpot" hat; a close-fitting, green, cutaway tailcoat; a yellowish waistcoat and a cravat; buff knee breeches, and gray woollen stockings, and on his feet were brogues. His clothes were clean and neat and in good condition. He was clean-shaven, his eyes were blue, and his hair light brown.

Nora completed her dressing, settled the child in her cot for the night, and went downstairs, determined to seek elucidation from the colonel at the first opportunity. After dinner she was able to draw him aside, and he listened to her recital with deep interest, for it was entirely new to him. As his wife was in a nervous state and, too, out of sympathy with Irish ways, he made Nora promise him that she would say nothing about it but would keep her eyes open and let him know at once if she saw anything more.

Meanwhile, he would make some enquiries himself, but in spite of all his efforts nothing further took place until about three weeks later, when Nora was about to leave for England. They were all having an early lunch, so that she could catch the train without rush, and the dining room was full. The colonel sat at the head of his table with Nora on his right, his wife at the foot, and the children disposed around it, while the two maids busily waited upon them.

Suddenly Nora turned to the colonel and said in a low voice, "He is here now. He is standing just behind you."

The colonel waited a moment lest he should attract too
much attention, and then turned round quickly, just in
time to see the little figure as it disappeared. It was standing quite close behind his chair, yet no one else had seen
it, and the maids must have brushed past it several times.
But nothing else happened and half an hour later Nora
left, never to return. Meanwhile, the colonel continued his
investigations steadily, his mind constantly puzzling over
this uncanny apparition, but without the slightest result.

Several months later he had occasion to visit an isolated part of his estate called Tooromin, driving there in
his trap early one afternoon. While there, he remembered
an old man of nearly ninety who had worked at the Big
House for his father and for his grandfather before him.
When he had finished his business, he went up to the old
man's house and, sitting opposite him before the open
hearth, he told his queer story. Old Michael sat silent for
some moments while his mind wandered back over the
years that were past and gone, then he slowly took his
pipe out of his mouth.

"That's a quare story, surely, Master Henry—quare indeed—but maybe I'll tell you one as quare." Then, without
hurry and with many a diversionary reminiscence, he told
how, when he was a boy of eighteen, he was brought over
to work at the Big House for a spell, sleeping of nights in
the barn.

One summer's evening, the day's work done, he was
leaning over the gate that led into the field in front of the
house, smoking his pipe before going round to the kitchen
for his meal of potatoes and buttermilk, when he noticed
a little man standing quietly in the field, not ten paces
from him. Though he had appeared, as it were, out of
nothing, he was so real and solid and was so clearly to be

seen that Michael never doubted his humanity for a moment.

The old man then painted a vivid mental picture of him—and it was exactly as Nora had described him and as the colonel had seen him.

Still leaning on the gate, Michael took his pipe from his mouth and bade him good evening in Irish, but the maneen made no answer. Then he spoke louder, and a third time louder still, but getting no response he tried in English. When that failed too, he became angry and cursed the little man fluently in Irish, whereupon he turned round, looked Michael full in the face, and vanished completely.

Speechless with astonishment, Michael stared into empty space for a few moments and then beat a hasty retreat to the kitchen. While he ate he told of his adventure, which was received with mild interest by the others, with the notable exception of one young girl, a maid in the house, who, with a toss of her head as she left the room, threw back casually over her shoulder, "Is it the little man that's in it? Sure I do be seeing him often." A few days later Michael returned to Tooromin and never heard more of the matter.

It is, perhaps, an unsatisfying little story, for it seems so incomplete, with its ends untidy and untied, but to me that makes it all the more real and impressive. It is only in novels that we have all the solutions ready to hand.

THE MOUNT LEINSTER FAIRY

The next tale comes from County Carlow, where rises gaunt Mount Leinster, dominating an area reputed to have a strong and active fairy population. By ancient tra-

dition they have always been powerful and busy on the
slopes and foothills of that steep mount and in the rocky,
rushy fields that stretch away from it.

I know an intelligent and educated lady, now elderly
and working in Dublin as a private nurse, whose home is
in that romantic district. Her people are fairly large
farmers near the small hamlet of Cranagh, which is three
miles from Borris, the nearest town. When she was a girl
of about nine, she had a very interesting "seeing" of a
fairy, an experience which she has never forgotten and
which today is as clear in her mind as on the evening it
took place over thirty-five years ago.

It happened one afternoon in November 1921 as she
went to bring home her father's cows. This was often her
duty when her brothers were not available. She had quite
a distance to go along the narrow twisting lanes, or bohereens, thick with mud in places, that led to the field of
rough sparse grass at the foot of the mountain where the
cows then were. The lane ended in the field, which was
enclosed by a tall grassy bank with a wide, low ditch on
the inside. It was between four and five when she reached
the gate, and there was a slight drizzle. The blue autumn
mists were already beginning to gather in the dips and
hollows of the rough ground. None the less, it was quite
light, as twilight had not yet begun and visibility was
normal up to fifty yards and more.

Having arrived, she opened the gate and stood back to
let the cows through. Usually they would all be crowded
round the gate, anxious to get in out of the cold and damp
and away from the scanty autumn grass to the warmth and
good feeding of the byre. But now only four cows stood
close to the gate, the other three being in a group some
twenty or more yards away. Having let the first lot pass,

she stepped into the field to get the other three, but they
came on at once, so she waited by the ditch to let them
go by. They were led by a gray one, a favorite of hers, and
it was not more than four or five paces from her when a
little fairy appeared from its far side. He looked fresh and
young, perhaps of her own age, and he moved quickly as if
he were in a hurry though not a desperate hurry. He
passed close in front of the cow, which tossed its head,
making a pass at him with its horns. As it did so he looked
round at it, in what seemed to her a friendly and posses-
sive way, and gave it a light tap on the nose with a switch
of sally which he carried in his right hand. He then
glanced quickly but intently at the girl, whom he almost
touched, and walking up to the ditch, took a long step
across it and disappeared right into the bank. He walked
into the solid earth with the same ease that a human being
would walk through a bead curtain.

Although, as I have said, it was misty and there was a
fine drizzle, the girl was easily able to take in every detail
of him clearly. About four and a half feet tall, he wore a
black cap turned up in front, which was rather like a sou'-
wester but neater, of much finer material and more closely
fitting, a bright red coat which was buttoned up in front,
and on his legs buff trews which seemed rather tight. The
sally switch in his hand must have been very recently
plucked, as there were still a couple of fresh leaves at the
tip.

She naturally was surprised and excited at seeing him,
and all the more at his vanishing, but not in the least
frightened. The cows had passed into the lane and she
found herself alone in the field, so there was nothing to
do but close the gate and make her way home with the
herd. As soon as she got home and was having her tea, she

told of her adventure, but she got little sympathy from her parents, and her brothers just laughed at her. In spite of all the scoffing, she has never been in doubt for one moment as to the absolute reality of what she saw.

THE LEPRECHAUN

Much the same experience befell a doctor I know who hailed in his youth from Foxford, a small town on the banks of the River Moy in Mayo, one of the finest salmon rivers in the country. On hot summer days the lads of the town used to bathe in a large pool in the river, not far from the lovely rapids. As some of the older boys indulged too much in rough horseplay and would even push the smaller boys into the center of the pool, where they were well out of their depth, my friend, who was then nine years old, and another boy about a year older would avoid them by going to a little pool they had discovered in a stream that flows from the Ox mountains on the eastern side of the town. At the foot of the hills, in a rough field dotted with great boulders and gorse bushes and wind-blown thorn trees, was the pool, which nowhere was deeper than a small boy's shoulders. It was partly sheltered by a clump of blackthorns and altogether was ideal for boys.

Late one afternoon the two lads bathed to their hearts' content, then chased each other to get dry. They dressed and began their leisurely stroll home, feeling at peace with all the world.

Before they had crossed the field, my friend saw a little figure dodge behind a big boulder on his left. He told his companion, who maintained that it must be a scarecrow flapping in the wind. But my friend was sure it was something very much alive, and to satisfy his curiosity they both walked up to the boulder to investigate. And what a surprise they got, for when they went round the boulder they found themselves looking at a little man about four feet high. He wore a cap that covered his hair, a close-fitting collarless black coat made of some good, shiny material like satin or silk and buttoned up tightly to his chin. He had a broad, rather flat face and he was clean-shaven except for curly brown whiskers, shot with gray, which ran round his chin from ear to ear.

He stood before them grinning in a most friendly way. The disarming, indeed inviting, friendliness of his smile impressed the boys specially, but that was not enough to calm their fears, for to them he was clearly a fairy, a leprechaun, a denizen of another world who had no place here, an unknown to be avoided desperately. So, after staring at him in stupefied wonder for some moments, they took to their heels and ran as if the devil himself were after them. They ran till they could run no more and were well away from the mountainy country and quite near the safety of the town and of other people. Then they sank exhausted to the ground.

When they got home they made no secret of what they had seen in that wild field and, indeed, they have talked it over together and among friends from time to time all their lives.

The doctor has assured me that the incident is just as clear to him as ever and that he could lead me to the exact boulder. He is a graduate of Trinity College, Dublin, and he served as a British officer in the first World War, campaigning in Salonica and France, and he is a man of intelligence and integrity.

THE CLONMILLAN SHEE

The next account I have is of a very different kind
of being. One might be tempted to classify it as a ghost
rather than an elemental, but taking everything into consideration I feel that it never was a human being but is
truly of the fairy world. My informant is Mr. Gowran, who
is today a prosperous owner of shops in Dublin, but who
hails from Offaly. The incident happened in 1901 when he
was a boy of ten.

Mr. Gowran's family lived at that time in the small
county town of Edenderry. One day in May, when the
cowslips were out and everything was bright and cheerful
with the promise of coming summer, he and a school
friend, eight-year-old Jack Gooley, set off for a stroll about
4:00 P.M. With two nine-year-old girls, Mary Gooley,
Jack's elder sister, and her friend Maggie Grehan, they
wandered along the road running north towards Mullingar. After going about a mile the girls, who were behind,
turned to the right along a lane which led fairly steeply
upwards to Clonmillan Hill. There was a farmhouse there,
where they were certain of refreshment from an aunt and
uncle of Mary's. They had been told to collect some buttermilk from them to take home for baking bread.

Clonmillan Hill has always had a reputation for being
connected with the fairies, including the great Shee as
well as the lesser Shee-og. A number of years before, some
man had ploughed up a small fairy ring or fort there, causing a good deal of discussion in the neighborhood, most
people deprecating the act as a trouble-making piece of
vandalism. I have heard that he died unexpectedly a few
years later. The farm lay halfway up the hill but to the far

side of it, and the lane, after going straight for some distance, turned to the left so as to reach the house.

The two girls had not got halfway up when the boys, who had only gone on a short distance down the Mullingar road, heard them call out. When the lads looked back they saw that the girls had stopped and were looking earnestly into the field on their right. After a few moments, they saw the girls turn back and run down the lane on to the main road again. On reaching the road, the girls went over to a gate opposite the lane and stared into the field beyond it. Then they began urgently beckoning to the boys to join them there. The boys, who were thirty or forty yards away, ran up at once, little dreaming what an extraordinary thing they were about to see.

When they joined the girls at the gate and looked through it, to their utter astonishment they saw, some forty yards away, a group of dark figures of human size standing in a circle about ten yards in diameter. Black capes or shawls were draped over their heads and hung across their shoulders and from there dropped straight down to or into the ground, but with no crease or bend where they reached it. The figures stood so close together that their draperies touched from their shoulders down, making it impossible to see past them. They were quite motionless, even to the folds and pleats of their draperies, as if carved out of some black stone, and their heads were erect. Mr. Gowran says emphatically that these black cloaks were not woollen but were made of some very fine cloth that is not shiny, and so could not have been silken either.

Another remarkable feature was that the whole center of the circle of figures appeared to be covered by a black cloth at the height of their shoulders. From it rose what seemed to be a chest—or, though the children did not think of it at the time, a coffin—and it, too, was covered by the same black material, which lay snugly on the chest and showed its shape clearly. The top of the chest was a foot or a little more above the heads of the surrounding figures. And on the top of this chest lay a set of old Irish bagpipes. Mr. Gowran can still describe them in detail and can remember just how they lay. There were three drones, each about three feet long, one of which lay towards him and the other two away from him. The bag and the mouth-piece hung down over the side of the box. The drones were of unusual shape and were as thick as a big man's wrist.

The children had stood looking at this curious sight for a considerable time, probably two or three minutes, when they saw Dan Jackson, the owner of the field, and his eighteen-year-old son approaching from the field beyond it, which was divided from it by a small ditch. The two men took long steps across the ditch and strolled unconcernedly on. It seemed as if they were going to walk up to the figures, but it was soon clear that neither of them saw anything unusual, and after passing within six feet of the dark, silent figures, they approached the gate.

Afraid of being asked awkward questions, and being rather alarmed at what they saw, the four children ran off towards the town just before the two men reached the gate. But the two boys, being bolder than the girls, stopped after they had gone a short distance and peered through the hedge again. They were now alongside the next field and so had to look through the side hedge as well, but they found a gap and saw that the mysterious figures were still quietly standing, but the circle had moved some ten yards further away and was now close to the ditch of the

next field, covering the track along which the two men had
just passed.

What were these eerie black figures that stood so still,
and what was the meaning of the bagpipes lying upon the
draped chest? The girls had first seen this silent group in
the field halfway up the lane and had called out. They had
then run back to the main road in fear, only to see exactly
the same sight again, for there were apparently the same
figures standing before them in this other field.

This sight has been seen by others round about, but
only at rare intervals of years, and the story of it persists
throughout the neighborhood. However, it was not till a
number of years later, when Mr. Gowran was a young
man, that his uncle told him that he also had seen the figures, a few years before the children had encountered
them. Locally, these apparitions are looked upon as fairies
and not as ghosts, and rightly so, I think. It has been suggested that they were members of the fairy hosts, perhaps
even the people of Bel, the great Celtic God who is honored with fires on May Eve—Beltane, as it should be
called—and that they lamented the passing of some special Celtic piper who had learned the fairy tunes to play
to them. However that may be, I feel they fit in much
more reasonably as fairy folk than as ghosts.

THE KILLEADEN FIGURES

I know of a rather similar case which happened to
a friend of mine some twenty years ago, not far from my
home. His name is Michael Sheehy, and at that time he
was studying shopkeeping so as to qualify for a post as the
manager of a cooperative store. It was cold and frosty
weather in January, and with a friend Sheehy had been

working late in the little town of Kiltimagh upon the annual accounts. At last, towards midnight, they put their books away and started on the four-mile walk home, for as far as the Killeaden Avenue gates their roads home lay together. They strode along vigorously in the bright cold night and soon crossed the bridge into the Killeaden lands. Just where the demesne land begins, a small road branches off past the "demon" tree (described in the next chapter) and runs with a wide detour round the estate, eventually passing the back avenue gate. But as they neared this point the two men stopped in some perplexity and awe, for they saw three figures standing in a group just where the byroad joins the highway.

And they were indeed three extraordinary figures. They were tall and well built and all were clothed in deep black. They stood close together and facing each other in a small circle or triangle, with their arms straight down by their sides and their heads bowed as if in sorrow or deep contemplation.

After some hesitation the two men plucked up their courage and walked past these eerie figures, but keeping as far away as possible, well on the grass verge on the other side of the road. Then they hurried on and parted at the avenue gates. The friend went straight on, but Sheehy—whose people for generations had been most respected tenants on the estate—walked as quickly as he could down the avenue, past the stables, along the back avenue, and out on to the road again which led to his home.

But as he reached the back avenue gate he stopped in horror, for there before him on the outside road were the same three weird figures, just as he had seen them before. It was, of course, quite impossible for them to have got

there by natural means. Even running, they could not have
made the detour in time, but there they were and in the
same queer poses as before. There was no other way home
so Sheehy, again keeping as far away as he could, ran past
them and made his way back as fast as he could go.

THE LIS ARD SHEE

To my mind, the most astonishing thing about this
incident is that no one else, as far as I know, had ever seen
these figures before. The nearest approach is the story that
old Martin Brennan, now dead these many years, told me
when I was a small boy. He was the head gardener at the
Big House in those prosperous days, and I was always a
special pet of his. He told me how, one summer's evening,
when he was working in the "outer blackground," a field
below Lis Ard, our famous fairy fort, he had looked up
and seen the bank lined with a score or more of the fairy
folk, all life-sized, the women mostly young and good looking and with shawls over their heads. The men wore red
or brown coats and some were bareheaded, with tousled
brown hair, while others wore conical hats set jauntily on
their heads. But all of them, both men and women, had
penetrating, staring eyes which even at the distance of
sixty or seventy yards seemed to pierce right through him
as he worked with his scythe cutting rushes. Altogether it
was a sight which made him retire hastily to the human
companionship of the farm buildings.

THE HAYTOR PIXIE

One of the most charming of these tales comes from
England and from an English lady, Mrs. C. Woods. Mrs.

Woods has one son, who had only recently passed through
his agricultural college when this event took place in June
1952. She is secretary of the Federation of Women's In-
stitutes for her county.

She and her son were staying in Newton Abbot. It was
her first holiday in Devon and it was glorious warm summer weather. The moors fascinated her, and though she
knew that some people think them dreary, cold and lonely,
to her they seemed alive and she spent much time on
them. On this particular day it was extraordinarily hot,
and she and her son had climbed to the top of Haytor, but
for some reason she wanted to walk down and back up
again by herself. Her son, lying under one of the great
boulders on the top, warned her not to go off the path lest
she disappear in a bog. So she duly promised and set off.
Going down was not too bad, although her arms were
burning from the heat, but climbing back took her some
time. She sat to rest on a "coffin" stone each time she came
to one. The path is lined with the large stones on either
side, set at intervals up the steep incline, at the top of
which are two very large lumps of stone.

She was at least three quarters of the way to the top
when she saw a little man standing against one of the
large boulders. He moved out from the rock and seemed
to be watching her, shading his eyes from the sun and
standing five or six yards out from the first of the large
boulders which form Haytor. She stared at him hard and
wondered. She felt a little afraid because, while sitting on
the various stones, she had wondered whether once people
had lived on the moor and if they really had rested the
coffins of their loved ones on the stones, and if so, whether
this little man resented her using them as resting places
too.

She looked up to the crest to try and see her son and hesitated whether to continue on her way or not. Eventually she went on, cautiously, and had got to within about forty yards of the little man when he turned away and dived out of sight under the boulder, Even so, she went the longest way round, lest he should jump out at her, and reached her son safely. He, of course, just laughed at her when she told him. However, she persuaded him to go down with her again to see if they could find him, and they went to the spot where he had disappeared. There was no hole behind the boulder and no undergrowth, nothing but quite short grass, so there was no place where he could have hidden. "It was no momentary sight," she says, "as I watched him for some time standing there, and I wondered what he was. I had no idea at first that he was a little man; I thought rather of some animal until I got much nearer, and then I just stared and said to myself, 'This is no animal, it is a tiny man in brown.' I felt and still feel so convinced."

She was able to describe him very well. He was dressed in what looked like a brown smock, with a cord or something like it round his waist. The smock came almost to his knees, and his legs appeared to be covered in some brown material. If he had anything on his head it was a flat brown cap, or else he had brown hair. He appeared to be three or four feet tall and gave the appearance of being elderly rather than young.

A WICKLOW FAIRY

Another recent "seeing" of a fairy was by a very charming and intelligent girl whom I know personally and who lives deep in the country in County Wicklow. In June

1951 she and her sister, then both in their teens, were
walking along a quiet country lane when suddenly a little
man appeared in front of them from nowhere. He was
standing in the road within a few feet of an old thorn tree
which grew out of the bank bordering the road. He stood
looking at them quietly but intently, and they stopped and
stared back in utter amazement. He was between two and
three feet high and was dressed all in black, with a black
cap, and he seemed to be youngish rather than old. One
girl said to the other: "Mercy, it's a fairy," and the other
replied: "The Lord save us, so it is." They became terri-
fied, and with trembling hands they quickly opened a gate
which was beside them and ran through it into a field.
Being good country girls, they instinctively closed the gate
behind them, and as they did so the little man turned
towards them, watching them closely all the time. Once
past the gate, they began to run through the field, but
they had not gone very far when they looked back to see
if he was still in sight. They could not see him about, but
they did see a very curious "something," about the size
and shape of a common tin kitchen clock, balanced on the
top bar of the gate. They then continued on their way to
the protection of their home.

It is interesting to note that at first the sisters had no
fear at all but only amazement; not till after several moments, when the reality that they were facing a fairy first
came upon them, did their curiosity turn to panic. Another
point is the curious object on the gate. Clearly it must have
had some connection with the fairy, but what, why, and
how quite baffles me. Though it was getting on for ten
o'clock in the evening the light was still quite good, for it
was twilight and the girls could see clearly and easily.

My friend had previously seen a little fairy in a wood

not far from her home, but that one was dressed in a bright-red coat. In the same wood she has also heard fairy music, with the pipes playing merrily and sweetly. As I write, I have before me her signed and witnessed statement concerning these incidents.

I have given a few firsthand accounts of visions seen by people of reason and reliability; with one exception, these people are alive today and are prepared at any time to reaffirm the truth and reality of what they have seen. And these fairy folk are romantic and friendly beings who, if they exist, can only make life more colorful for us. Some of the ancient Fathers of the Church have taught that all these beings are fallen angels, but that they have fallen in different degrees, some heavily, some lightly. If this be so, then I feel sure that these friendly and harmless "gentle people" have fallen a very short way indeed.

THE FAIRY IN THE FIREPLACE

Tradition fully supports some modern experiences which suggest that there are household spirits, or fairies, as well as country ones, and the old names make it clear that they have been in our folk history since the dim past. Thus Ireland has her Cluricauns, the small sprites who sit by the hob and look after, and even at times tidy, the kitchen by night.

Here is an experience which surely must be of this kind. It is related by a lady whom I have known all my life and who is intelligent and most upright. Hearing I was interested in these things, she has sent me an account of it.

A number of years ago, when she was a child of five, this lady, who is of Irish descent though born in England,

saw a little man under charming circumstances. The incident took place, surprisingly, in Wandsworth, an inner
suburb of London. This little girl, whom we will call Vicki,
even at that age was passionately devoted to dancing. She
was already having lessons and she used to practice and
improvise whenever she could. A friend of the family, Dr.
Hamilton, was staying in the house at the time. He was
known to the little children as Hamperlum, which was the
best they could make of his name. He was a good pianist
and delighted in the children. One afternoon, on going into
the drawing room, he found Vicki by herself sedulously
practicing her steps. To encourage her to continue, he sat
down at the piano and played suitable music for her to
dance to and generally to spread her pretty little self. She
was wearing a small, short white frock, and Dr. Hamilton
was charmed as he watched her tiny toes tripping about
and the unassuming natural grace of her movements, her
wee body in perfect rhythm with her feet. But after a time
he had to go about his own affairs and he went off, leaving
the little tot to herself.

But Vicki did not mind in the least being left alone, and
she continued intently with her dancing. After a while she
tired and stopped and, still standing on the floor near the
piano, she idly looked round the room. It was early summer, and though the maids had laid the fire, it was not lit
nor would it be until the cool of the evening, if even then.
But when her eyes reached the fireplace, which was at the
far end of the room from where she was standing, she was
amazed and thrilled to see, sitting on the round cobbled
coals, a little figure perched happily with his legs crossed
like a tailor's. He filled the fireplace all right and seemed to
be a bit more than half the size of the child.

At once Vicki thought, "Oh! Hamperlum has given me

a dolly, how *lovely!* I've never seen one like this before."
So she slowly tiptoed down the room, and when she got
near enough, right up to the fender, she knelt down and
held out her wee hands to lift up this lovely present from
off the round smooth coals. But the next moment she had
stopped, spellbound, for the little man, who was all dressed
in green and wore a red "jelly-bag" cap, smiled and nodded
his head several times, and his smile was quite the most
friendly and attractive smile she had ever seen. But, alas,
having made this friendly gesture, he quite suddenly disappeared completely.

At first, poor Vicki nearly wept with vexation and dis-
appointment, but she soon recovered, for somehow she felt
that the nice little man was still about and was as friendly
as ever. Her heart went out to him without reserve. She
said nothing about him to anyone but cherished him always as a precious secret to be kept strictly to herself. Indeed it was not till she was quite grown up that she even
mentioned the affair to a few intimates. I do not think I
can do better in conclusion than to quote Vicki's own
words as she ends her letter: "I can see it all very clearly
and vividly now at this moment. I *know* he was a little
Pixie man and he was a *good* Pixie because he made me
feel happy."

CHAPTER III

Fairy Trees

Respect the tree and let it be,
From branch to root, nor touch its fruit!
Of itself the tree did grow,
From a dog who long ago,
Enchanted by the fairies' power,
Was buried here in mystic hour;
Therefore we bid you let it stand,
And if you follow the command
You will be happy all your days,
But woe to him who disobeys!
C. G. Leland

Except perhaps for raths, duns, and lisses—the fairy forts of legend—nothing in Ireland is more closely associated with the fairy folk than are certain types of tree. Wherever one goes in the country one does not have far to look to see some lone thorn bush growing in a field. The thorn bush is locally reputed to be under fairy protection, but there are many popular misconceptions about the tree, and inaccurate generalities have too often crept into those versions of local folklore which are held by people not close enough to the earth and to the earth folk to distinguish between fact and fiction.

It is, for instance, widely thought that only the whitethorn is sacred to the fairies, and that all whitethorns growing alone in the center of a field are "fairy trees." Indeed, many people include in this category all whitethorns, even when growing in a hedge, provided only that they have a sturdy and fairly venerable appearance; but the whitethorn, although it is the most usual and most popular with the earth folk, by no means has a monopoly of fairy patronage, for it shares that honor with several other kinds of tree. In Ireland its greatest rivals are, in order of merit, the hazel, the blackthorn, the bourtree—which is the English elder—the sally, the alder, the ash, the holly, the birch, the oak—especially a twisted mountain oak—the broom, and the Scots fir; also, to my personal knowledge in at least two instances, the rowan or mountain ash, in spite of its being usually associated with white-magic properties. In addition to all these, although it is a plant, the golden-flowered buacalan bui, or ragwort, must be given a place of importance.

In Scotland they have also the juniper and ivy, but I have not heard of these in such a way in Ireland.

The hazel, one of the most important of all, goes back in Irish mythology to an honored place in the dim mists of the past. Then the hazel nut was the repository of all knowledge, as was the apple in Eden. No wonder the ancient gods and the spirits of today are reputed to revere and care for it. Of the other trees, the fairies do well in cherishing the blackthorn, for it is one of the loveliest trees

in the Irish countryside, especially in early spring when
its masses of bright, white flowers contrast so strongly with
its yet-leafless black twigs; and the toughness of its
branches is proverbial.

The bourtree, so often looked upon as a weed, is also
worthy of esteem for its many good qualities. Indeed, its
various parts have more medicinal virtues than any other
tree or plant. John Evelyn, the famous diarist, emphasizes
this in his *Sylva*. Its berries, too, are famous for wine and
are a truly God-sent winter food for that gentle form of
life the fairies love, the birds. The sally is another tree of
ancient use to man, giving us our baskets and panniers and
the background of our thatching, while the fairies themselves weave and plait the withies cunningly. The alder,
one of the catkin-bearing trees, is best of all in its resist-
ance to water and wet rot, and ancient lake dwellers were
dependent upon it. In the fairy world the water spirits and
the mysterious white horses from lake and deep pool like
and protect it especially.

Then come "oak, ash, and thorn." Need one say more,
for Kipling knew his fairy lore well when he wrote of
them in *Puck of Pook's Hill*. But when they are a trilogy
like that, they are really more concerned in witchcraft than
with fairies. Birch and broom are two lovely trees and can,
when in suitable places, be adopted by the fairy folk. The
Scots fir, with its lovely bluish-green spindles blending in
satisfying harmony with the purple red of its bark, is always a delight to the eye, and a wind-blown tree or a small
group of them can well be a haunt of fairies. The rowan is
a lovely tree, too, and I cannot understand how it obtained
its reputation as anti-earth folk; for centuries it has been
widely used as a protection against witches and their
spells, and, indeed, against all spirits. Yet I know of one in

North Clare which was locally looked upon as a very special fairy tree, and again there were three or four growing
close together on the eastern slopes of the Galtee mountains which I was firmly assured by many people when I
was there in 1921 was the haunt of some very nasty demons.

The fairy folk are quite discriminating in their choice
of trees, and the site of each tree is an important matter.
Whether the seed has only fallen into its place through the
normal accidents of nature, or has been deliberately but
supernaturally planted for the purpose of the folk, none
among mere mortals can tell—and the answer is, after all,
unimportant. However, there are many positive signs to
enlighten the interested enquirer and, in some cases, to
show which of them are surely fairy trees, though the final
test must always lie in ancient local tradition. Any of the
trees mentioned above as being connected with the fairies
can, when growing *within*—or, even more so, when growing *on*—the surrounding back of a rath or dun, be assur-
edly looked upon as under their special protection.

Any tree at all which is growing inside a fairy ring can
be taken as certainly an important one to them—and so
can a thorn, black or white, a hazel, a bourtree, a holly, or
a broom, when growing strongly near to a ring or, if in a
rocky field of rough tufted grass, near to a big boulder or
to a welling spring. If the tree leans towards the ring or
boulder, or over the spring, it is an even surer sign. The
lone thorn growing in the middle of a rough and stony
field, or on a sharp hillside, is much more likely to be "protected" and in use by the little people than is one in an
ordinary, well-tended farming field. Of course, the mere
fact that the young plant has survived the hazards of

grazing cattle, of heat and frost, of drought and flood, and
of man's plow and spade, may well suggest some magic
help—but not necessarily so; and the little people are undoubtedly not too deeply interested in some of the lone
trees in fields and banks.

THE KILLEADEN FAIRY THORN

There are several fairy forts in the neighborhood of
my home. One in particular, Lis Ard, which is a perfect
circle perched on top of a steep hill and crowned by a
thick clump of tall beech trees which can be seen for miles,
is famed far and wide. Raftery, the blind Irish poet, sang
of it and of his home fort, nearby Ard Righ. In my grandfather's time a thorn tree grew on the northern side of the
surrounding bank and was by nature very curiously
shaped for, perched upon its four-foot-high stem, the
branches lay cleanly, flat and round and neat, just the
shape of a grindstone, some four feet across and a foot or
more thick. This was without question an important fairy
tree and it was revered as such by all who knew it. My
grandfather, after many years abroad, had at that time, I
think, lost touch and sympathy with Irish folk tradition,
which in those "practical" and unimaginative Victorian
times was very much frowned upon in British and pro-
British Irish circles, with which my family then identified
itself.

Whatever the reason, he decided that the little fairy
tree would be nicely ornamental in front of the house.
However, when he tried to get it moved he met with unexpected difficulties, for no man in the place would put a
hand to it, in spite of all the personal affection which they

had for the "little master." But, small in stature though he
was, he was a very determined character and so, nothing
daunted and ignoring all the forebodings of the countryside, he set to work manfully and moved it himself.

This was in 1851, and it thrived from the beginning in
its new site and is flourishing there today; but, whether it
was a coincidence or not, for the next few years he had
great trouble in his farming and, with otherwise unaccountable bad luck, he lost both stock and money heavily.
Other things which have happened during the passing
years have been put to the account of this tree, and there
is now a strong suggestion locally that it should be returned to its proper fairy site. It may well be doubted if
such a move is possible, in view of its great age.

In my young days it still retained its original shape, but
during the first World War it got out of hand in spite of
clipping, and it is now taller and conical—the shape of a
toadstool rather than a mushroom. I remember well how
the donkeys we used to ride bareback when we were small
had a perverse habit of trotting under it, where they would
just fit, causing us to be swept off their backs, no doubt to
their great satisfaction as well as to the amusement of any
fairies that might be supposed to be watching.

In recent years the tree has afforded a safe home, first
for wrens and then for robins, both of whom are "fairy"
birds, and they have reared families in it with cheeky
boldness. Indeed, when some two years ago the robins
took over from the wrens, the latter had the impertinence
to build their nest in a jasmine bush which trailed across
the lintel of the porch and to within three inches of the
top of the hall door. If anyone dared to stand in the doorway, especially when smoking, the parent wrens would
flutter about the fairy tree and a low garden wall on the

other side of the door, twittering and chirping in a frenzy
of indignation until one had the tact to move away.

"OAK, ASH, AND THORN"

In the field in front of the house there is a great
oak, by far the oldest tree in the place, with huge, sweeping lower branches upon which generations of the family
have swung when children. Close by it is an ancient thorn,
one of the largest and oldest I have ever seen, and in perfect health too, while just beyond is a vigorous ash, making
the fairy trilogy of oak, ash, and thorn. Many is the time
in years gone by, as boy and youth, that I have slipped
out by the light of the waxing moon to gather a twig of
each and bind the ends with threads of bright scarlet wool
as a protection against any hostile spirits of the night.

On the slopes of Lis Ard there are three other authentic and venerable fairy thorns; and under an old spreading
oak at the foot of the hill is reputedly a place for their
meetings and dances at certain times of the year, though
I never discovered just when these times were. I heard
most of these tales when I was a child and moved freely
among all the people; but I was, I suppose, too shy or too
scatterbrained to ask the questions that today I would
want so much to ask and to have answered. However, the
tales of fairy trees are innumerable and can be gathered
anywhere.

A DEMON TREE

It is not only the fairies who have a lien upon our
trees, for sometimes these are appropriated by more sinister figures—by poltergeists and elementals and demons—

who deal out fear and hurt to those who incur their displeasure; or who, even unwittingly, approach them too closely.

I know of one tree which has a peculiarly malevolent surrounding. In reality there are three trees, two thorns and a bourtree, but they look like one—for the three straight stems are almost touching, certainly not more than two inches apart, and their branches are inextricably mingled into one bushy crown. Growing up these stems are a couple of thick briar shoots, which throw out tendrils through the branches and add sharp teeth to the prickly points of the thorns, so that the bush is quite impenetrable except for small birds and field mice. This tree is set in a low-lying field of poorish land and some thirty feet in from a narrow country road, so that one looks down on it as one passes.

It is guarded by three malevolent demons who, after dark, haunt that stretch of the road. There are eerie and disturbing tales round about of passers-by in the late of the night who have had their arms fiercely gripped so that the marks could be seen next day, or who have heard blood-chilling, inhuman laughs or angry spittings as if from some enormous cat; and sometimes even dim and horribly misshapen figures have been made out moving in the darkness.

One afternoon, not long ago, I visited the tree and took three berries from it as my due—but that is quite another tale. As I examined it, I noticed that someone had had the temerity to attack it seriously, for there were three or four cuts from an axe all close together on one of the three stems. However, the tough wood had withstood the onslaught well; only a small chip had gone, the scars had weathered brown, and moss had grown in places, showing that it must have been some years ago that the "sacrilege" had been committed.

I have often since wondered who did it, and what perchance has happened to him since. I believe that with carefully placed enquiries I may yet find out.

ROADSIDE FAIRY TREES

Here are two cases of hostile spirits appropriating thorn trees growing beside a well-used high road. On the south side of the road that leads westwards from the town of Kiltimagh past the cemetery towards Balla there are two old thorn trees, each of which has a queer reputation. The first of them grows out of the bank little more than two hundred yards from the town, while the second is a good deal further along and stands just in the field behind the bank.

Some fifty years ago the parish was ruled, and very autocratically, by a remarkable man of outstanding character and ability. He was Father Denis O'Hara, and in his sincere love for the poor he did great good, but by his somewhat brusque and forceful methods he sometimes inadvertently caused offense and put nerves on edge. In 1908 a Mr. Barton, a businessman living near the town for a few years, had on several occasions clashed with Father O'Hara and generally felt irritated and on edge with him. Mr. Barton too could be quite outspoken when he felt strongly about anything.

One evening, after Mr. Barton had been discussing his grievances at length in the town and had done so with a good deal of heat, he set out for home after a final stirrup cup. He had nearly a mile to walk, as the house he stayed in lay beyond the cemetery on the Balla road, but shortly

after he had started he met a friend and stopped to talk
with him. It was a fine summer evening and not a leaf
stirred in the quiet still air as they stood under the first
thorn tree I have mentioned. Very soon the conversation
came round to his special grievance and he began to pro-
claim in no uncertain terms what he thought of the
worthy parish priest. Not getting from his friend the sympathy to which he felt he was entitled, he became more
vehement and ended up by exclaiming indignantly, "May
the Devil take him to hell out of this!" Thereupon there
was a rush as of wind in the thorn tree above them, and
they turned to see it bending down and swaying under a
terrific gust which roared through it, and yet there was no
wind at all, not even a gentle breeze, and the air around
them was as still and quiet as ever. As soon as they realized
this extraordinary happening, the two men promptly took
to their heels, Mr. Barton making for his house and his
friend running into the town. There he went straight to
Mr. Murphy's shop and related it all to him, and it is Mr.
Murphy himself who has related it to me.

The friend was steady and reliable and was absolutely
sober and in control of himself as he spoke to Mr. Murphy;
besides, having just run up, he had had no time to invent
such a curious story. Mr. Barton himself corroborated it all
in every detail afterwards, and his rather shamefaced attitude showed him all the more sincere.

Mr. Murphy also recounts an incident regarding the
other tree, in which he himself was involved. Mr. Murphy,
now in his late eighties, has always lived a frugal and ab-
stemious life. Throughout his youth and early manhood
he was a keen athlete and took a considerable amount of
exercise to keep himself fit. Even when, in his thirties, he
had given up organized games, he continued to take exer-

cise and often went for a spin or a smart walk along the country roads in the evening after the day's work was done.

On this occasion he was out for a walk with a friend, and they happened after a while to stop for a few moments as they continued some discussion. Suddenly Mr. Murphy felt a sense of strong, overpowering hostility to himself, which seemed to envelop him as closely as though a cloak were wrapped around him. He turned quickly in the direction from which it seemed to come and realized it was pouring out from a large thorn tree which overshadowed them.

This hostility, this feeling of vicious, bitter evil, as he describes it, gripped him so relentlessly that he could not even speak, for he was numbed and paralyzed by it. After a few moments of this helpless horror his companion, who had also been quite silent, seized him by the arm and, murmuring, "Come along," dragged him into the middle of the road and began to walk him rapidly back towards the town. After striding along for some time without speaking, his friend at last blurted out, "I don't know whether I am talking nonsense or not, but I felt something horrible in that tree in the field where we were talking. I just could not stand it, and that's why I pulled you along so suddenly."

Mr. Murphy did not take long, for his part, in assuring him that he himself had felt exactly the same. Up to that time Mr. Murphy had never heard anything about that particular tree, but since then it has transpired that over many years people have occasionally had much the same experiences. Curiously enough, some have not connected with the tree the manifestations they have had but in a vague way have just blamed that section of the road. All the same, the tree's unpleasant reputation has for a long time been known as far away as Killeaden and Treenabontry, four and five miles away from it.

The Thorn Tree on the Bank

Fairies will protect their trees, often giving sharp foretastes of worse to come to those who threaten them or even interfere with them. It is also said that if thorn trees grow close together, especially three of them, they can be dangerous to get involved with in a way that does not fully recognize the fairies and their paramountcy over them. This is all the more so when three or more grow naturally close together so as to form an angle in the shape of an L or V.

Here is a case of a warning. The private lane that runs by John Solon's house from the road to the fields of his farm on Killeaden is enclosed on each side by a grassy bank. One day some forty years ago John decided to widen the lane near the house and so he began to dig away part of the bank. Nearly opposite his house there was—and still is—a small thorn tree growing out of the bank. All went well and John busily took away cartloads of earth till he got near to the tree. He then suddenly became ill and was forced to stop work, but he did not yet associate this in any way with the tree. Within a couple of days he was fully recovered and he set to work on the lane again, first tackling the further end of the widening he was making. After some time he moved up to the other end, near to the tree, but as soon as he did so he became ill again and was forced to stop. This happened two or three times more until he became aware without any possible shadow of doubt that his threat to disturb the little tree was the cause

of it all. As soon as he realized this he left it severely alone,
nor would he allow anybody else to interfere with it afterwards. The tree, which was old and small at that time, has
since begun to grow and is now quite large.

THE COTTAGE HOSPITAL

To destroy a real fairy tree is firmly looked upon as
extremely dangerous if not fatal, and many are the stories
of swift retribution, though some years may pass before
the debt of "sacrilege" is inevitably paid. One wonders
whether these things can all be mere coincidences or
whether there is in fact a real cause and effect running
through them.

Here is a curious case within my personal knowledge,
every detail of which can be verified by the curious without difficulty. It concerns the same town of Kiltimagh and
occurred in 1920 or thereabouts, when that outstanding,
respected parish priest, Monsignor Denis O'Hara, as he
was then, was presiding over his flock with an earnest desire for their material and spiritual welfare. For a long
time he had felt that the sick needed more done for them,
and he at length decided to have a cottage hospital built
to serve the neighborhood. He approached the govern-
ment and received a substantial grant in aid and was able,
without difficulty, to find the rest of the cost from chari-
tably disposed parishioners.

With his usual energy he set to work to get his project
brought to fruition without delay. The architect's plans
were passed and a site was chosen at the eastern end of
the town, where a field was bought.

Up to this, all had progressed with speed and smoothness and without any noticeable hitch, but now the story changed, for there happened to be two lone fairy thorns growing in this field and, no matter how one might try, it was quite impossible to fit the little hospital in without cutting one or other of them. Neither the parish priest nor the Dublin architect was prepared to pander to "this fairy nonsense" for a moment, so the hospital was sited in the most convenient spot, covering one of the thorn trees. But, to his disgust, Father Denis, in spite of his prestige and authority and the respect and affection in which he was held, found it difficult to find anyone willing to cut the tree; all those approached made excuses or bluntly refused. At last, he persuaded a man who lived not far outside the town, beyond the site of the hospital, to do the deed. He was a decent orderly man, always ready to do odd jobs about the town and to give help when required.

After having a few drinks to fortify himself, he duly cut the tree one afternoon, and as he walked along the main street of the town to the presbytery at the other end to report the carrying out of his work, the lads of the town laughingly called out a warning to him. Sturdily confident, he shouted back: "I'll be back, never fear, and to hell with your bloody fairies."

But, alas, that very night he had a bad stroke from which he never recovered. For something over a year, he hobbled on two sticks about his little house, a hopeless cripple, and then he died. So he did return to the town eventually, but in a coffin on his way to the cemetery which lay at the other side of it.

The work had continued vigorously all the time and the hospital was built, yet it was never opened. Everything occurred to hinder it, and in spite of all that could be done the idea of a hospital had to be abandoned. Ever since, the little building has been the local barracks of the Civic Guards, and the other tree still flourishes in the grounds. *Sic transit gloria mundi.*

CHAPTER IV

The Pooka

I who has sought afar from earth
  The Faery land to meet,
Now find content within its girth
  And wonder nigh my feet.

                    AE

          I find the Pooka a difficult
spirit to define or even to name in a satisfying way, for so
many experts use many different forms of the name and
describe many different appearances and behaviors of this
spirit. Its exact type seems peculiar to Ireland, but the
form in which it appears can vary so from place to place,
from century to century, and even from person to person
that it can easily become quite bewildering. Its tradition is
widespread and it crops up in the old tales in many forms:
a pony, an ass, a dog, a horse, a bull, a goat and, according to Yeats, even as an eagle. Whatever form it is in, it

must be jet black and with blazing fiery eyes, though
these are not always so conspicuous. But no matter how it
appears, it is always in some animal form and I have never
heard of it as a human. Yet an affinity between it and the
English Puck is also claimed. In Irish the name surely de-
rives from *puc*, a buck goat.

This Pooka spirit is famous throughout Ireland, and
though it and good English Puck certainly have very
similar names, the two earth spirits have fundamental
differences in character, for the Irish Pooka is much
tougher and rougher than friendly English Puck, who at
his worst is only amusingly mischievous, while the Pooka
can, if it will, be frightening and harmful in its exploits,
which then have little of the fun of Puck's gay pranks.
Brewer's *Dictionary of Phrase and Fable* describes the
Pooka as wholly malevolent, often fatally so, but that is a
gross libel on the Irish spirit. Admittedly, it can certainly
be pretty fierce and nasty if it is not treated properly, but
in all the old traditional tales, if it is met in a friendly and
respectful way, it will be friendly and even helpful in
return.

The many tales about the Pooka which Dougles Hyde
and William Butler Yeats collected and published are, I
think, more in the nature of nursery stories, based perhaps
on some old occurrence which has since been embroidered
beyond recognition to provide an amusing tale for the
children gathered round the hearth of an evening. The
story of "The Piper and the Puca," translated from
the Irish by Hyde, is an obvious case in point. In this tale
the Pooka is an ass, is closely linked with the fairies, and
speaks as a human. In it, also, the gold coins given to the
piper turn into dried leaves in the morning. This meta-
morphosis was universal in the tales and trials of witches

all over Europe throughout the Middle Ages and must be of great antiquity.

In the story of the Kildare Pooka in *Irish Fairy and Folk Tales,* edited by Yeats, it again appears as an ass, but on this occasion a most accommodating one, doing all the kitchenmaid's work each night. This is more like a friendly cluricaun or a Scottish brownie or glaistig and does not sound a bit like the real Pooka, so it must be classed as another nursery story.

In the fascinating series of broadcasts from the Northern Ireland B.B.C. a few years ago, entitled "The Fairy Faith," some very convincing recent stories of the Pooka were given, in which it appeared as a black pony with shaggy mane and sturdy body and, as is essential when they are seen, with blazing eyes. This is its usual form in Ulster, and though there are tales of it in this form from all over the country, I have never come across one firsthand. Outside Ulster everyone I have met who claims to have seen the Pooka has seen it as a great black dog, with curious tail very thick at the base and coming quickly to a sharp point at the tip.

As a pony the Pooka is reputed to delight in waylaying belated home-going revelers, offering them a lift home on its back, then taking them for wild and terrifying gallops over hill and dale, eventually upsetting them into a ditch far from their destination. As a dog it is usually much more peaceable, though it will also sometimes threaten and frighten.

John Players, Ltd., when issuing a series of cigarette cards of Irish place names some years ago, included one of Poulaphuca, the lovely waterfall in the Wicklow Hills, with the following description: "Polla' Phuca means 'The Pool of the Pooka.' The Pooka being an Irish fairy well

known in England under the name of Puck. In Ireland he
is an odd mixture of merriment and malignity, and his
exploits form the subject of innumerable legendary tales.
He often appears in the shape of a black dog, sometimes
as a donkey. He is often lurking in Raths and Lisses,
hence there are many old forts in the country called
Lissaphuca and Rath Phuca. The best-known place bear-
ing his name is Poulaphuca, among the Wicklow mountains, where the River Liffey falls over a ledge into a
deep pool."

Apart from identifying it too fully with Puck, this is
a well-satisfying short description of it.

Among the Pooka's general activities it is reputed to
make a point of breathing on all blackberries on "November Eve," as Hallowe'en is called, and so making them
from that time on unfit for humans to eat.

Here is a selection of firsthand tales by people who
have encountered this rather fearsome black fairy dog, all
of whom are alive today and, I am glad to say, none the
worse for their rather startling experiences. This shows, I
feel, that our friend the Pooka, though far from being
what one might call a pet, is not really as bad as it has
sometimes been painted.

The Derry Pooka

A friend of mine, Mr. Martin, who was a prominent
civil servant in the East till he retired at the general
hand-over after the war, had a particularly interesting
encounter with the Pooka when he was a young man. His
father, a retired regular colonel, lived in their old home
in County Derry, and my friend was at this time completing his course for a degree at Trinity College, Dublin.

It was in 1928, his last year at college, for he was to go
up for his finals in June. At Easter he went home for a
short holiday. It had been a very dry, warm spring, and
the local river, only a few hundred yards from his house,
was exceptionally low.

One sunny afternoon he went down to the river to
try for a trout. As he was standing on the dry, gravelly
edge of the bed, casting into a small pool, he suddenly
felt constrained to look to his right along the river. He
could not see far, as there was a bend less than a hundred
yards away, and there the hedge of the next field ran
down to the bank. But as he looked he saw a huge black
animal come in sight, padding along in the shallow
water. He could not at first make out what it was, whether
dog, panther, or what, but he felt it to be intensely menacing, so without wasting a moment he dropped his rod
and jumped for the nearest tree on the bank, a youngish
ash, and climbed till it bent dangerously with his weight.

Meanwhile, the animal continued padding steadily
along, and as it passed it looked up at him with almost
human intelligence and bared its teeth with a mixture of
snarl and jeering grin. His flesh crept as he stared back
into its fearsome, blazing red eyes, which seemed like
live coals inside the monstrous head. Even so, he could
only think of it as a wild, savage animal which had,
presumably, escaped from some traveling circus.

It passed on and was soon lost to view round the next
bend, and once he felt it was well on its way, he slid
down from his precarious perch, grabbed his rod, and
raced back to his house. His father was out, but he got
his shotgun, loaded it with the heaviest shot he could
find, and went off in search of the animal, feeling that no
one in the neighborhood would be safe while it was still at

large. However, he drew a blank. Everyone he met, including those who must have been in its path, denied all knowledge of the animal.

Eventually he returned home and told his father of his adventure. Both were thoroughly puzzled as to what it could possibly have been. The next morning he returned to Trinity and forgot all about it. He got his degree in June and then went home. Shortly after returning, he opened a new packet of cigarettes one afternoon, and before taking out a cigarette he threw the card away. As he did so a bell rang in his mind and he quickly picked up the card. On it he saw a very lifelike picture of the animal. The card was one of a series of Irish place names and it showed Poulaphuca with the famous waterfall in the background. In the foreground was the Pooka itself, the great black fairy dog.

After he had told me this story, I managed to get a copy of this card and I showed it to him. "Yes," he said, "that is just what I saw, except that it does not show the red eyes or the slavering mouth and wicked teeth. It was as tall as a mantelpiece. That picture is so true you'd think it was drawn from life."

Until he saw the cigarette card he had had no idea that it might have been something occult, but now he started making closer enquiries among the local people and soon got plenty of information. It was quite well known, and there were a number of stories of its having been seen over the years, usually standing in or by the river near the local bridge, but always in the gloaming. He was told too that it was fifty or more years since anyone had claimed to have seen it in full daylight. He heard little more about it, for he soon qualified for a post abroad and left for the East in a short time.

THE BALLAGHADEREEN POOKA

A few weeks after hearing this story from my friend, I happened to visit an office in the city in the course of business. The man I wanted was late, and while waiting for him, I chatted with his secretary, a charming and pretty girl and intelligent too. She told me her parents were farmers some three miles from Ballaghadereen in County Roscommon.

"But that is near me, for I am from outside Kiltimagh, in the heart of a fairy country," I said, laughing.

"Oh, we have fairies, too," she replied, full of local patriotism.

"Ah, my dear, I am sure they are not as real and tough as ours," I maintained.

"But I've seen one," she blurted out in indignant tone. Then she stopped, embarrassed by her admission. This, of course, fired my interests, and I soon convinced her of my sympathy, and once she was sure I would not laugh she readily and convincingly told me her tale.

It was at her home, about 6:00 P.M. on a hot summer's afternoon some six years before, when she was sixteen. She was standing in a field just behind the house when she noticed an enormous black dog as high as her shoulder walking by her only three or four yards away. As it passed it turned its head and looked at her, though with interest rather than hostility, but to her its eyes seemed almost human in their intelligence. She had no thought that it was supernatural nor even any sense of nervousness until it reached an iron gate opening into the next field, some twenty yards from where she stood. Then, to her stunned horror, she saw it quietly and without hesitation walk clean through the closed gate as if the solid iron were merely mist.

For a few moments she remained rooted to the spot, the hair at the back of her neck tingling and rising, then she pulled herself together and, turning, ran screaming into the house to the protection of her mother. She received little sympathy in that quarter, for as soon as her mother was able to make out from her panting phrases what had upset her, she told the girl sharply not to be silly. As the daughter persisted in maintaining the truth of her story, the mother then and there chastised her soundly. Profiting by that experience, she took good care to be reticent afterwards, and only some of her closest confidantes ever heard the story. None the less, it has remained in her mind as clearly as if it had happened the day before. I showed her the cigarette card, and she agreed that it was just what she had seen.

A GALWAY POOKA

My schoolmaster has seen the Pooka, but that was some years ago, when he was a young man. He was staying in a house in the small north Galway town of Ballygar in 1913. Having been far into the country one day, he was cycling to the town in the gloaming when he found he was being followed by a large black dog. It loped behind him, looking up at him in a way that made him feel uneasy, though even today he finds it difficult to explain why. As he cycled on, he became more and more ill at ease, his nerves unaccountably taut, till at last, to his intense relief, as he crossed a small culvert the dog stopped and left him to go on alone. Although he had had a feeling of the eerie the whole time, he did not

think of it as in any way unnatural; but when he got home
and told his host of his adventure with "the big black
dog," he found a very different complexion, and a very
convincing one, put upon it.

The "dog" was well known in the neighborhood, for it
had long haunted that particular stretch of country, and
most people avoided passing that way after dark unless
in company. A number of men and women had seen it,
and to some of them it had appeared only to disappear
into nothing before their eyes, though no harm had been
known to come to anyone.

A PONTOON POOKA

The Pooka is to be found even nearer to my home,
for it frequents the ancient woods of stunted oak and
holly on the western shores of Lough Conn, and especially
the lovely winding road that runs between Lough Conn
and Lough Cullen to the south. The whole of this wild and
beautiful area is an ideal and satisfying setting for the
home—and for occasional appearances to humans—of
such romantic spirits as the Pooka and of leprechauns,
cluricauns, and the rest of the Shee-og, the little people,
whose lives are woven into the very earth itself. Excepting
only the lone, bare pile of great Nephin, towering in
mystic majesty more than two thousand feet above the
surrounding plain, this countryside, though it has beauty
and to spare, has not the grandeur nor the awe-inspiring
power suitable for the great Clanns of the true Sidhe
(Shee) themselves, or for their gods and goddesses of
Nature who rule the land from their secret abodes.

An old man—he must be well over seventy today—
who was born and bred between the two loughs, told me

how well he remembered that when he was young no one,
alone after midnight, would cross the bridge at Pontoon
which divides the two loughs, because of the great black
dog that haunted the bridge and the road and country to
the west. It was to be seen at any time after 12:00 o'clock
at night and would come bounding out of the woods to
glower at the belated wayfarer. But the old man, having
been settled in a town some miles away for the past sixty
years, and not being sufficiently curious, had heard nothing
of it since.

I was staying this Yuletide with my sister in her compact and cozy little red-tiled house which stands on a
knap of rock between these very woods and the lough.
The house, overlooked on the west by Crockmor Hill and,
beyond that again, by the rugged heather-clad and
granite-strewn steeps of tall Larrigan, is on the road to
Crossmolina and about a mile beyond Pontoon. The
stream that runs by it, under Corryoslar bridge, is full of
lovely water lilies bright with white and golden flowers
in June. Everywhere the wildest life abounds: plant, fish,
bird, and animal.

Primed by the old man's statement, I began discreet
enquiries among the local people and at once got positive
results. This part of the country has been heavily de-
populated by emigration to the industrial centers of
England, but both among those who have stayed and
those who have returned I received the same response.
This was that the Pooka is well known here and can be
met with almost any night. Some said it would more
likely be seen during the waxing of the moon, however.
Even the boys and girls knew of it, and one man, the
vigorous father of a family living in a little house a mile
"be east the bridge," and half that distance from the

bigger of the two hotels, told me of an encounter with it some years ago.

Late one summer's night, on his way home from the older and smaller of the hotels, he stopped to pump his cycle just short of the bridge. As he pumped away, a large black dog jumped lightly over the wall from the dark woods and stood looking down at him. He had no doubt of its fairy nature and—saying a fervent prayer to the Blessed Virgin for protection—he jumped on his cycle, soft though the tire yet was, and pedaled away vigorously. It did not follow him, and he was soon over the bridge and past the big hotel, reaching with thankful relief the safety of his own house.

AGAIN THE PONTOON POOKA

Some twenty-five years ago, the Pooka was seen on the same road, this time just west of the Pontoon Bridge Hotel. My informant is a highly educated lady of substance and responsibility, well known and respected far and wide round that part of Mayo.

On this occasion she was strolling down the road in the early evening, accompanied by her setter dog. She suddenly noticed a black object lying in the center of the road, some twenty yards in front of her. At first she thought it was a donkey, but as she looked it got up and then she saw it was a very large black dog. The dog looked at her, slowly walked to the side of the road, and stepped on to the short heather and coarse grass beside it, but as it did so, it suddenly disappeared. One might say that she just lost sight of it, but if so, where could it have gone? For there was no place where it could hide. And the behavior of her own dog was remarkable too. Though not an aggressive animal, it was plucky enough and always ready to maintain its rights in the face of any strange dog. It had been ranging about, and at the time the lady saw the Pooka on the road her dog was about the same distance from her but to her left, nosing about on the grass. It first noticed the Pooka as it stood up but, instead of showing the proper interest that one dog should show in another, the dog at once ran to its mistress with every sign of fear, its tail between its legs as it trembled close to her heels. It remained so, whining for the few moments till the Pooka stepped off the road and disappeared. At once its signs of fear vanished and it continued nosing about as if nothing had happened. The lady is in no doubt that it was, indeed, the local Pooka which she encountered, and the behavior of her dog seems conclusive.

A WICKLOW POOKA

In 1952 a friend of mine, Margo Ryan, a charming and very intelligent girl, encountered the Pooka in a way that is typical. It happened within a day or two of midsummer and though it was nearly midnight, by summer time of course—astronomically about 10:30 P.M. to 10:45 P.M., for we are twenty minutes behind England—it was reasonably light.

She was carrying home a large can of buttermilk from a neighboring farm and was walking along a quiet country road within a short distance of her house, which is near Redcross in County Wicklow. As she strolled on in the quiet of the country night, a quiet that town people and people in mechanized country districts can never know, she heard a soft patter behind her and the next moment an enormous jet-black dog ranged up alongside and walked quietly on in company with her. After a bit, as it seemed so peaceable and friendly, she put out her hand to pat it, without looking down. But she could not feel it; her hand seemed to miss it and touch nothing. So she tried again, but again she could not touch it.

This puzzled Margo, so she looked, and there it was, as solid as solid could be, though it had now moved a little away to her left and just out of reach. A moment later it was close to her again, so again she tried to pat it, but with as little success as ever. This startled her a little and she turned her head so as to look at it fully, but as she did so it moved forward and continued walking just a few feet ahead of her in the middle of the road for another fifty yards or more when it stopped, turned its head to the left, and vanished into thin air as she was looking at it. Let there be no doubt about it whatever; it did not run off but actually vanished from where it stood in the center of the road. Besides, at that place there was a ditch and bank with no gap where a dog could have gone.

Margo then realized vividly that the great dog stood much higher than her hand, which was at her side, and it was not possible for her to miss it. Her hand *must* have gone through it as if it were air.

After this, her nervousness turned to positive fear, and she hurried home as quickly as she could without spilling the buttermilk. Her family received the story of her adventure with interest and all sympathy, for they are well aware of the reality of these things.

This Pooka was obviously a friendly one, for it made no attempt to upset her but was just companionable, for a short distance. Indeed it behaved much the same as those that I have already described in Ballygar and Pontoon.

These few firsthand cases of the appearance of the Pooka provide some points of interest. They show, for instance, the wide range of country which it covers, for it is equally at home in the running water of the streams, by the still waters of a lough, in woods and fields, or on well-used highways; the advent of the motor car seems to have made no difference to it. Another feature is that it appears as readily in the full light of day as it does by night or in the gloaming, and as readily to old as to young.

The skeptics may say that the Pooka is just an ordinary dog, probably a Labrador retriever, which is a common breed in the country, and that the nervous imagination of a semi-educated and perhaps festive peasant has exaggerated it absurdly, even if in all good faith.

It is quite true that Labradors are fairly common in Ireland, but because of this very fact the country people are thoroughly aware of what they look like and are therefore the less likely to be mistaken. Countrymen too, especially today, are a shrewd and level-headed breed, and not at all the gullible dupes that "superior" people from the towns so often paint them. Let our town friends try to buy a cow in a country fair and they will not be likely to underestimate the intelligence and natural psychology of the small farmer.

Besides, in most of the cases I have given, the observers were educated persons of well-known and reputable families, all of them seeing the apparition by daylight and all quite emphatic to this day that what they saw was no natural dog; and when I suggested a Labrador to them, they laughed the possibility to scorn.

One word of warning will avoid an easy misconception. In English and Scottish witchcraft, as well as in Con-

tinental, a black dog, though rarely of great size, is a
common occurrence as a witch's familiar or as an imp
servant of the local devil. But these more sinister spirits
have no connection whatsoever with the Pooka dog, any
more than has good English Puck with the seamier aspects
of black magic. No, the Pooka is an entity in itself and,
with some patriotism, we in Ireland like to think of it as of
good Celtic stock and to feel that its connection or blood
relationship with the spirits of other lands is at best a
distant one.

CHAPTER V

Magic Cures

Speak not—whisper not;
Here blowest thyme and bergamot;
Softly on the evening hour
Sweet herbs their spices shower.
Walter de la Mare

The cures which I give in this chapter are wholly magic and can be carried out only by someone who has in some way obtained the specific power to do so. There is no other explanation for these cures but a magical one. As I see it, there is no halfway house between accepting a magical explanation and maintaining that the facts are all wrong or that the cure did not take place. I am satisfied that the details, where they are not matters of my own observation, were given to me by my various informants in all sincerity. For the rest, the reader must make up his own mind.

"RINGWORM"

Early in January 1956 I personally saw and closely observed a remarkable cure which, to my mind, can rightly be classified only as pure and genuine magic. This affair has been witnessed and attested by many highly reliable, educated, and responsible people, and every detail given here is factual.

I was staying with my sister at the time in her lovely little house on the western shore of Lough Conn. We had planned to have a few friends in to dine one evening, and my sister asked a girl from a local cottage, who often helped her in an emergency, to come in and assist her maid to wait and wash up and do all the various household chores which arise on these occasions. The girl, Agnes, unexpectedly refused, saying that she had a bad leg. There was a man "beyant below the mountain," she said, who had a certain cure, but it must be done on a Thursday or a Monday. Her leg, she added, was so very painful that she could not wait the four days till next Monday, for today was Thursday.

My sister had counted on the girl's help, and her flat refusal was very awkward; there was no one within reach who could readily be got to take her place, for many of the local girls had gone to England. So I intervened, and as a compromise I offered to drive Agnes to this man for her cure and then to bring her back in time to help during dinner. Happily, she agreed; driving would save her a two-mile journey on a bicycle over rough and narrow roads which would not be pleasant with such a painful leg. I, for my part, being interested in these things, was glad to get the chance of seeing what kind of "cure" it was. I must admit that I was entirely skeptical, for the girl's complete confidence did not seem to me to make sense.

Before taking her, I had a careful look at her leg, which my sister, who in her day had been a distinguished nurse, had also thoroughly examined. My sister had no doubt of the nonsense of the whole thing, but, living in the West, she has long since learned to have great patience with local prejudice and contrary customs.

In examining the leg, I found that it was, indeed, a nasty place. Just above the right ankle and on top of the shin bone there was a large swelling, a carbuncle, much larger than a duck's egg, and the center had burst and was pouring filthy yellow pus. All round this open place the flesh for more than half an inch was an unhealthy yellow blue, while on each side of the leg two new spots, red, angry circles, were developing which looked to me like the beginnings of bad ringworm. In the normal way, after suppurating for some time, it would burst and the bad core of muck would come out. If it did not then get worse and the infection did not spread, it might slowly mend over the course of several months. The girl had already suffered from it for over two months as it gradually worked up to its present intolerably bad and painful state. Having seen it, I felt doubly sure that nothing short of expert and up-to-date medical treatment would do her any good, and the idea that a rough peasant had any quick and certain "cure," no matter what herbs he used or complicated applications he put on, was asking too much of one's credulity.

However, everyone being willing, I started off with the girl, and after a drive along as narrow and difficult little bohereens as I have known, we came at last to the neat

thatched and whitewashed cottage where the man lived.
I saw that there was just room enough to turn the car in
a kind of midden yard beside it.

We got out, and the woman of the house, who was
about thirty and gave the impression of being thoroughly
practical, sensible, and mentally alert, came out to meet
us. As soon as she heard what was required, "Yes," she
said, "himself can do it all right, for it is a Thursday, but
he is presently away, out on the bog with some other men.
But I'll send the colleen with you to right you the way."

But then a small gossoon some twelve years old came
forward and said it had to be done with earth from a
particular bank about twenty yards away, on the side of a
still smaller bohereen leading downhill to some fields. A
number of curiously wind-twisted whitethorns grew along
the top of it here and there in a ragged sort of way. He
ran over to it and scraped up with his bare hands a small
handful of apparently quite ordinary brown earth, which
his mother wrapped in a piece of paper and gave to her
daughter.

I turned the car and off we drove again, out on to a
byroad beside a small lough. In due course we came to
a bog which stretched away before us in black and purple
shades towards great cloud-capped Nephin some two
miles northwards. There, close to the road, were five or
six men with a horse and cart mending a soft track that
ran across it. I stopped well short of them and let the
colleen go ahead to talk with her father. He then came
striding up to the car, opened the door, and gave a quick
but searching look at the leg, which Agnes had meanwhile put forward for him, announcing that he could cure
it. He asked me to turn the car and stop a hundred or so
yards away, presumably so as to be out of range of the

observation of the other men. "I'll do it behind the car," he added, as if to emphasize the point.

In imminent danger of going into one or other of the deep bog ditches on either side of the narrow road, I managed to get the car turned and to drive to the place he had indicated. Having come so far, I was determined to see everything that was done, and do so as thoroughly as possible. I got out and stood by the rear bumper, facing inwards towards the left side of the road, making Agnes stand next to me while the little colleen took up her station just behind us.

The man wasted no time as he came, stepping up in a purposeful and matter-of-fact way. He held out his hand to his daughter for the parcel and knelt on his right knee before Agnes, emptying the earth from the paper on to the closely cropped grass verge before us.

Then the "cure" began. First he spat on the palm of his right hand, pressed it on the little heap of earth before him, and then, having done this three times, placed his hand upon the bad spot on the girl's leg. (I have rarely seen a rougher or more horny hand creased and lined with the grime of honest labor.) He rubbed it lightly for a couple of seconds, for all the world as if he were feeling a horse's fetlock for spavin. This process he repeated three times, so that, in all, he did nine spits and nine presses on the earth and three rubs of the leg. Watching extremely closely, I can affirm with certainty that there was never any visible sign of a spit on his palm, nor did any visible amount of the special earth adhere to it; spits and presses must have been purely symbolical. He stood up, saying to Agnes in a matter-of-fact way, "Come again on Monday and then on next Thursday and you will be cured." With that, he shrugged his shoulders, turned, and strode off abruptly without taking the slightest further notice of us.

As we drove home, I became more and more irritated
and indignant as I thought of the trouble I had gone to
and the expectation I had had of seeing some really
interesting rite surviving from the dim past, or perhaps a
new use of country herbs of which anyone else could
make use. Instead, there had only been this meaningless
mumbo-jumbo, which had scarcely lasted more than a few
seconds. However, it was some satisfaction to have got the
girl back in time to do all that was required of her. After
dinner, that evening, having told the story of my expedi-
tion, I showed Agnes's leg to two of the less squeamish
guests; the next day, during a small cocktail party, two or
three who were interested also had a good look at it.

On Sunday I found Agnes eating a meal in the kitchen
when I looked in for something, and I asked her how she
was. Though she stoutly asserted that it felt much better
already and that all the pain had gone, I was not particularly impressed, as the painlessness could be accounted
for by self-suggestion, especially as she had been so very
confident all along; and, for that matter, so had the man
and all his family.

Agnes was up at the house again on Wednesday,
having paid her second visit to the man the previous
Monday. Hearing she was there, I went out to the kitchen
to see her.

"Well, Agnes," I said, laughing and ready to deride her
faith in the absurd proceedings, "I suppose your poor leg
is much the same. You had better let the doctor have
a try at it now."

"No, sir," she replied, smiling back at me triumphantly;
"it is nearly well already, and it will be quite all right in
another few days."

"Nonsense!" I said, indignantly. "Just let me look at it and see."

She put her foot on a chair so that I could look at it closely. As I bent over I got a shock of surprise which I am not likely to forget for a long time. The girl was quite right, for her leg *was* nearly cured! Instead of the foul yellow pus there was a clean-looking scab. The blue flesh had changed to a healthy pink, there was only a very little swelling where five days before it had been larger than the largest egg, while the two side places with their angry rings had vanished completely.

I had nothing to say. All I could do was to look and look, but however much I looked I could find neither any flaw in the cure nor any explanation for it. I called my sister and could not help smiling at her very understandable but entirely friendly and amused sense of outrage that anything should so defy all the accepted usages and precepts of medicine.

I saw the leg for the last time on the next Sunday, the day before I left for Dublin. Having been treated by the man for the third and final time, Agnes's leg was completely cured but for a dry and rapidly disappearing scab a little larger than a shilling. A few days later my sister wrote to say that even the scab had gone and there was no sign of anything except a scar which will always be there, a permanent proof of her illness and the cure for it that can be seen today.

It may well be argued that proper medical treatment could have got just as good a result. That may be so, indeed I am quite sure it is so, but I doubt very much if it could have accomplished it as smoothly and swiftly. Even if one does accept that claim, medical treatment could scarcely have done it faster, while on the other hand

our local cure cost absolutely nothing, either directly or
indirectly, and it involved no costly drugs, instruments, or
treatment. From whatever angle one looks at it, one must
admit in all fairness that this local cure comes out best.

The tradition in regard to these curious powers is
particularly interesting and is to be found, with various
local peculiarities, up and down the western districts of
Ireland. It would be interesting to know if similar traditions are to be found in other countries, whether now or
in the past. Here, these powers are usually but not invariably handed down from father to son or from mother
to daughter, and if passed on outside the immediate
family they must at least be kept within the same sex. The
only exception to this rule that I have ever heard of was
in the case of two women in the townland of Bohola, only
a few miles from my home. These women were sisters,
and when the second one lay dying she passed her power,
or did her best to do so, on to her nephew, who lived some
fifteen miles away. But from what I heard at the time and
have since heard, I doubt very much if that transfer was
at all successful.

In this case of curing "ringworm," the power must be
passed to an unbaptized baby, and words which cannot be
divulged but which are in Irish are whispered into the
child's ear after an ordinary garden worm has been
placed in its hand.

There are some points worthy of notice in this rite, for
the fact that this occult power can only be given to an unbaptized infant, in spite of the fact that all the adults
concerned will be fervent and practicing Catholics, shows
that the custom must go back to pre-Christian times.
Again, if the baby is going to receive the power effectively, the worm will die instantly, the moment it is placed

in its palm. If it does not die, then the transfer has failed and the baby will have no power of healing. And with these simple country folk, all ailments of the skin, or just under it, are bundled together under the general heading of "ringworm," which is prevalent in some districts. To demonstrate further the looseness of their terms in this respect, it may be noted that the common earthworm is made to do duty for the minute ringworm. As the child grows up, it realizes that it has or will have this power, though many consider that it is latent and cannot be used until the death of the giver. In this way, these powers are passed on through centuries.

In parts of Ireland the ringworm cure is so much an accepted matter of fact that I know of one country doctor in the north midlands who always sends sufferers from it to a certain local "wise woman" who has the "cure," for he says that she can cure quickly and certainly in a way that no doctor can.

THE ART OF SEWING

In the wild country lying to the south of Nephin there is a gift which consists in an intense love of and skill in needlework of all kinds. This, naturally, is the pre-rogative of women and it is passed on in much the same way as the ringworm cure, only in this case a threaded needle instead of a worm is placed in the unbaptized babe's hand when the appropriate Gaelic spell is muttered.

There is an amusing story told in this connection. Some five or six years ago an old woman from this wild district died at the age of seventy-two. She had this power of needlework, and all her life she busied herself at it with love and skill whenever she had the slightest opportunity. But, astonishingly, she was entirely *cithog*, or left-handed at it, nor could she bear to have a needle in her right hand. These details are undeniable facts and the story accounting for them is delightful.

It appears that when she was born her mother was most anxious that the newly arrived daughter should have this gift. As there was an elderly woman in the neighborhood who possessed it, the mother sent for her and urged her to endow her child with it. But for some reason the woman was reluctant to do so. However, the mother kept plying her with poteen, the country home-distilled and most potent spirit, until at last she consented. But by then her body was as much affected as her will by this powerful alcohol; and heavy with drink as she was, she was every moment becoming more shaken. However, determined to see it through, the mother handed her a threaded needle, guided her tottering steps over to the baby in its crib, and then retired to the other end of the cabin, as it is not lawful for anyone else to hear the spell. But, alas, so fuddled had the woman become that by mistake she put the needle into the babe's left hand instead of into its right, and thus it grew up left-handed for sewing though thoroughly right-handed for everything else.

GRIT IN EYES

Like Queen Victoria in her later years, my old grandmother, on the rare occasions when she felt impelled by charity or duty to visit some outlying part of her estate, used to do so in a sedate bathchair drawn by a well-groomed and overfed gray donkey called Nessa. Her constant attendant on the progresses was a short but tough hunchback, Martin Groak, who was a special pet as well as rather a butt for us children at the Big House.

Martin, dressed in his best for the affair, would lead the donkey, while either the estate bailiff, black-bearded and genial John Solon, or the herd, John Gill, would stalk with heavy-footed dignity beside the chair. Martin Groak could hardly have been more than four feet six inches tall, but he would grasp the bridle firmly and look about him with an expression of undaunted courage as if he were skillfully and bravely managing an unbroken colt of the worst and most vicious kind, though I doubt if anything short of a charge of dynamite would have made that quiet old donkey do more than look mildly surprised.

Martin and his old mother, Biddy Cosgary, lived in a large room built in ancient times under the stone steps leading up to the harness room and the granaries, and it is about her that I have my story to tell. To us, Biddy seemed ageless, at any rate she seemed to have stayed the same age an unconscionably long time, and no one we ever asked had known her to be any different. She wore the typical old-fashioned clothes of those days, now gone fifty years almost, the most conspicuous of which were a heavy home-spun woollen shawl over her head and shoulders and wide, voluminous skirts. Indoors she wore a little frilly white cotton cap, closely fitting over her head and with two cotton strings tied in a bow beneath her chin. The lined and wrinkled brown skin of her old face was in striking contrast to the neat white cap and her sharp, twinkling gimlet eyes. Her thin lips gave an impression of uncanny power, wielded, however, with a sense of humor. Though not exactly looked upon by the countryside as a witch, she was none the less reputed to know things and to have powers denied to more ordinary people. Therefore she was treated with a deference which

her social position among them by no means warranted
of itself.

To many people, her curious powers were not a mere
matter of repute but of very real and practical fact. One
of these powers used most openly was that of curing eyes,
especially of removing any foreign body that had got
under one's eyelids. Now, many country cures are practical
medicinal processes, depending on some unsuspected
drug or therapeutic treatment which has merely antici-
pated modern discoveries, often by centuries, even when
their use is overlaid with various mystic rites. But there
was no such thing with Biddy Cosgary's cures of eyes, for
her methods were blatant magic, and nothing but magic.

In a kind of bay off the avenue at home, and within
twenty yards of the granary steps, there is a very ancient
spring bubbling out of rock some six feet below the level
of the road. From time immemorial it has been covered in
with stone work built into and through the wall of the
adjoining orchard, under which there are worn stone
steps leading down to the crystal-clear spring. Indeed,
it may well be that five hundred years ago the old Francis-
cans who then owned all the land wisely placed their con-
ventual farmhouse on the site where the Big House stands
today, for the convenience of that lovely water. Behind, in
the orchard, with its great branches overspreading it
protectively, stands a huge patriarchal ash tree, while
before it lies a big low trough carved by long-vanished
hands out of a single block of stone.

Biddy Cosgary always used the water from this
ancient well for her magic cures, and her formula of action
was almost always the same. When anyone came to her
in distress with something in his eyes, she did not necessarily consent to help him, but if she did decide to do so

she set to work without delay. She took a cup and a saucer, one in each hand, and went to the well. She filled the cup there and, returning, placed the full cup on the table on her right and the empty saucer near it but more to her left. She sat down, making her client sit opposite her, on the other side of the table. She would never lay a hand on him or touch him in any way, only requiring that he should look at her as well as he could, even through his streaming eye. She then took a good sip of the water from the cup, rolled it round inside her mouth, and mumbled words—spells, presumably—which no one was ever able to make out. Having done this for a short time, she would bend forward and put the water from her mouth out into the saucer. There, floating in the water or sinking to the bottom, would be the foreign body out of her client's eye. Of course, she did not, nor did she claim to, cure the hurt already done to the eye by the grit or whatever else it was. She merely removed the offending matter, and the rest was properly left to the ordinary healing processes of nature.

Two people, one of whom I know to be alive today and the other of whom I believe to be, were cured by her and can verify every detail. The first is John S., then serving as footman in the Big House, who later became our coachman. Later still he entered the Royal Irish Constabulary and only retired on the disbandment of that force in 1922. Since then he has lived with his family on a farm not far from Castlebar and can be seen there today. As a young man he went to Biddy with a very nasty bit of sharp grit in his eye. All efforts in the house to get it out in the ordinary way with the tips of handkerchiefs, oil, and such like having dismally failed, he went in desperation to see Biddy. But he went without much confidence, for from his environment at work and his developing education he was very inclined to ridicule such things.

However, Biddy was in a friendly mood and she soon had him put to rights. His astonishment was intense when he saw the little speck in the saucer and found no further hurt in his eye. But when he thanked her she waved him aside, telling him he did not deserve to be helped when he had shown such little faith in her as to come to her only as a last resort.

The other patient was a young girl on the estate, who would now be an elderly married woman. But she married out of the neighborhood, and I do not know where she is living. The story today is that she got a louse in her eye and Biddy removed it at once in her usual way. But I always heard as a boy that it was not a louse but a grass tick which, having fastened itself on the eyeball, had swollen in a very painful way. As is well known, if a grass tick is pulled off, it leaves its fangs—and its head—in the flesh, which then festers. When de-ticking a pet, we children always used to burn a tick's back with a lighted match, which made it let go completely. However, in my version Biddy got it out and into the water in her saucer quite intact and with nothing left in the eye.

But she had no monopoly on this cure. A younger woman, Bridget Walsh, who lived in the townland of Polronahan, two miles away across the river, performed the same cure and was even reputed to be able to do so from a distance. She flourished ten or fifteen years later than our friend, and because they overlapped for a few years only, there was not the war of witchcraft between them as happened in Lancashire in 1612 between Anne Chattox and Elizabeth Demdike.

Bridget Walsh's fame spread so far that the parish priest went out to interrogate her as to which powers she invoked, those of heaven or those of hell. Whether truthfully or not, she succeeded in convincing him that what she muttered in Gaelic over her water was invariably a Christian prayer and not a pagan spell. But I have a shrewd suspicion that, when pressed, all "wise" persons as a matter of elementary self-protection will, indeed must, assert indignantly that they use a Christian prayer and not a pagan spell, no matter what it is they really use. This may sound cynical, but it must be remembered that nearly all these cures are a great deal older than Christianity and cannot be in the least dependent on it or on its prayers for their efficacy. The cures will have been Christianized later for the sake of respectability and to conform with the new universal public opinion.

Biddy Cosgary Speaks

In 1902 my aunt Emma interviewed Mrs. Groak, generally known to the people by her maiden name of

Biddy Cosgary, about her cure of eyes, and she took down verbatim what the old woman said. I have this original account in my aunt's own hand by me now as I write, and it requires a little explanation. When my aunt was a baby, she acquired the affectionate diminutive of "Timmie," which arose from the efforts of her younger brothers and sisters to pronounce her name. This stuck to her all her life in the family and with some of the female tenants who were her contemporaries or who had worked in the Big House when she was small, and they often continued it with respectful affection. One of these was Mrs. Groak, who in 1902 was a widow living in one room under the granary steps. Her hunchback son was undergardener and man-of-all-work about the house.

Knowing how highly religious my aunts were, and even more so my grandmother who ruled all, high and low, as a benevolent autocrat, old Biddy was at pains to make her art "white" and not "black," so the Virgin Mary was introduced to the charm and the original heathen goddess was tactfully changed into the entirely mythical "Saint of the Eye" in heaven. The word "thraneen," which she uses, means a blade of grass. When she says, "You may do it nine times," she means that it can be done only on the two magic days of Thursday and Monday. It can be done three times together on either day, and if it does not work then, it can be repeated three times on each of the two succeeding magic days.

I should dearly like to know to whom, if to anyone, she passed on her powers on her deathbed. Certainly not to her son Martin. After her death I never heard of anyone else having it in our neighborhood except Biddy Walsh from Polronahan across the river; she definitely possessed it before Biddy Cosgary died.

Here is my aunt's account, which she took down just as Biddy Cosgary spoke it.

" 'Tis the dirtiest charrum ever I done. I'd not like to be doin' it for everyone. Rayson why, whatever's in the eye will come out in your mouth. And isn't it strange the clergy's don't like us to be doin' it. There was one Father Quin, a curate, and I made my confession to him once. ' 'Tis all prayers, Father,' says I, 'to the Blessed Virgin and the Saint of the Eye.' 'Well, I'm not stopping you,' says he, 'you can do that for me,' says he. But some of them wouldn't like you to be doin' anything with a charrum. There was one man living near a chapel and he had a charrum for the head fayver. But I don't believe in that charrum. They missures round your head with a band. So they leaves the band on thin and they has a great deal of worruds and prayers to be said. But I study into it this ways. Sure all that's givin' that head fayver is a foul stomach by using different kinds of food and not getting any clearin' out.

"Well, Miss Timmie, my charrum is given from a man to a woman and from a woman to a man. 'Tis only praying to the Blessed Virgin and the Saint of the Eye. Sure, yis, there is a Saint of the Eye up in heaven. Well, when anyone come to me, a good neighbor or a well wisher and so forth, and ask me would I cure the eye for thim, thin I should bring a drop of spring water from the well and to take it in my mouth, Miss Timmie, and to kape me mouth closed and say those prayers and worruds to the Blessed Virgin and the Saint of the Eye. Then, savin' your presence, I let the water down out of me mouth into a white plate and you'll see in that water whatever injury is in the eye. And to do that three times. It mightn't come the first time. You may do it nine times, and if the person is worthy you'll see it at last some of the nine times. Monday and Thursday are the days. There might come two Mondays and one Thursday or two Thursdays and one Monday, it don't matter which.

"I could do it for you and you over in England. They comes to me from all sides. There did a letter come over out of England to me and told me that a young boy I knew, when he was saving hay, got something into his eye and that hurted it and the eye was keeping bad. Well, I tuck and done the charrum for him. And the first drop of water I let down out of me mouth what was in it but a big piece of grass. And the boy wrote over agin that he knew well the day and the hour I done the charrum. He put a great roar out of himself when the thraneen was leaving the eye, by raysin it hurted him grately.

"There did come a man up to me out of Strade for me to cure his eye. Well, Miss Timmie, the first drop of water I let down out of me mouth, what was in it but all blood. Raysin why, the scum that gathered in the eye was bad blood."

It will be noticed that Biddy said the power is passed on from a man to a woman or from a woman to a man. This is contrary to what I have heard and may be only an exception. But one cannot be too dogmatic about these things.

FOR MEGRIM AND HEADACHES OF ALL KINDS

There is one cure which Biddy Cosgary had no power to perform, and concerning which she displayed professional jealousy in her talk with my aunt.

The ancient procedure of "measuring the head" is a power held by people who have received it from relatives of the previous generation. As far back as I can remember, an old woman called Nancy White, who died in 1915 at the age of seventy, successfully practiced this art. It is a "white" art, not a "black" one, for great good was done by it to many people and no one was ever harmed. Another woman, who lived till recently near Turlough, some eleven miles from my home, also had this good power, but she left the district a few years ago.

However, a fit and healthy seventy-two-year-old man now living not far from Nephin does this healing work for any local person who is distraught with headaches. For his protection I shall call him Sean Kinahan, and I shall withhold details of the road to his little cottage. All the same, he is well worth a visit for anyone who needs his help.

As with most cures in Mayo, one must go only on special days of the week, in his case Tuesdays and Thursdays, and one must receive the treatment on each of three consecutive "visiting" days. His technique of measuring is the same as old Nancy White's; like her, he uses almost anything to "measure" with, a cord, a tape, or a bit of cloth, and he does it in two directions. First he draws the cord across the forehead, making the two ends meet at the back of the head so that it is closely fitting but not tight enough to be unpleasant, and holds it in position for a minute or two. Then he measures the head from bottom to top: he starts at the chin, draws the cord upwards over each cheek just in front of the ears, and makes the ends meet at the highest point of the head. But all the time that he is measuring in each direction, the tips of his fingers are pressing firmly and feeling, feeling, as if he were searching out the weak spots. Even when he has finished "measuring," he gives the head another firm pressure with both hands and the proceedings are complete.

WARTS

Claims to cure warts are very widespread and astonishingly varied in their composition. There is a world of difference between the cure of warts by Mark Twain's Tom Sawyer and Huck Finn, who discuss the relative merits of a dead cat or "spunk" water in a rotten tree bowl, with the added solemnities of spells and awesome midnight rituals, and the persons in Ireland who still "buy" the warts at any time for a penny. But this latter method is often ineffective and may well infect the buyer himself, especially if the warts are of a tough and nasty kind.

Most doctors now accept the fact that there is something deeply psychological about warts which is not yet fully understood; following this line of thought, many of them will put the cures down to suggestion. How this explanation can stand, in view of the undoubted fact that cures are sometimes carried out by these apparently psychic means without the knowledge of the patient, it is difficult to understand.

Here is an exceedingly interesting case of a cure which is authenticated beyond the possibility of doubt.

The daughter of a leading family in one of the northeastern counties of the Republic of Ireland, who was then about eighteen, had been afflicted for a number of years by a bad outbreak of unusually strong and virulent warts upon her knees. Her parents tried everything, taking her to specialists and dermatologists in Dublin, England, and America, without the slightest success.

Finally they consulted a lady friend of mine, who is also a friend of theirs, with an uncanny magic power of curing warts. She can do other curious things, including water divining. I have no doubt that in the good old days of the early seventeenth century she would have been burned as a witch, in spite of the fact that very many people have good reason to bless her kindness and the help of her curious power, and no one has ever had cause to rue it. When, despairing of orthodox methods, the parents, though rather skeptically, appealed to this friendly "white witch," she readily agreed to help. She went up to their house one sunny summer afternoon and inspected the warts.

Nothing daunted by seeing how bad and strong they were, she went into the vegetable garden, where she plucked and opened two broad beans. She threw away the beans and returned with the shells to the drawing room. There she set to work, rubbing the fluffy inside part of a shell lightly upon each wart. There were so many warts that she thought it advisable to use two bean shells instead of only one, lest one should wear out.

Having done the process carefully to the end, my friend handed the bean shells to the girl, who took them immediately to the garden, as instructed, and buried them. And so the matter was completed, for, as the bean pods rotted, the warts fell off and disappeared, never to return again. Within four days there was not a sign of a wart anywhere. As the cook expressed it with delightful imagery, "Sure, they pattered off her like hailstones!" That was some years ago, and there has not been a sign of a wart since, nor will there ever be.

Some interesting points may be noticed in this cure. In the first place, it is the patient and not the curer who must bury the bean pods. This shows, surely, that there must be some subconscious unity between the two. An-

other unusual feature is that when my friend feels that
the cure may be difficult, she likes to pluck the bean pods
early and carry them about on her person for several
days before using them, as she feels this makes them much
more powerful. Having to use fresh bean pods confines her
wart activity to the summer months. Imported out-of-
season broad beans might do as well, but that has yet to
be tested.

CHAPTER VI

Pranks and Mischief

There came a satyr creeping through the wood,
His hair fell on his breast, his legs were slim;
His eyes were dancing wickedly, he stood,
He peeped about on every side of him.
                                        James Stephens

We all know well what imp-
ishness is when applied to a child, but let us now see
what it really is when coming from the originators of the
term, the imps themselves. I give here some examples of
it, though several of the occurrences described in other
chapters, such as the stray sod and the fairy hunger,
might well qualify for a place here, too. Of these examples
I will only comment that the first two seem to arise from
a mild resentment at a local trespass, while the others are
clearly just fun.

THE BUTTER

It is well known to right-minded country people who have a proper sense of what is due to a neighbor that when one lives in fairy territory, even when one only spends a night there in passing, one should pay some friendly tribute to the unseen world about one before settling down for the night. And so the wise housewife will leave a sup of milk or a saucer of stirabout or a bit of soda bread beside the hearth or even perhaps outside the cottage door before she retires. This custom is widespread, and I have seen it done in India and have heard of it in West Africa. While I was in Germany after the war I saw staid Westphalian farmers, starting out for a day's shooting, whether the game was duck or deer, go up to the first cow they met in a field and draw a sup of milk from it, only an eggcupful or so, on to the grass. When I remarked on it they would say, "Zum glück" ("It is for luck"). If I pressed them, they would admit that it was done to propitiate the local nature spirits so that the sport would not be interfered with and the game protected. I am sorry I was not more interested at the time and that my knowledge of German was not better, or I would have found out exactly what kind of earth folk they visualized.

Irish fairies don't seem to be so interested in blood sports, but all the same they are liable to play tricks or just take what is to hand if they do not get the tribute or attention they feel they are entitled to.

One very well authenticated case concerns an incident which happened some years ago to two friends of mine, Mr. T. Coleman and his wife. Mr. Coleman is a prominent

professional man in Dublin and his wife is well known in
Dublin society as a very charming hostess. The event I
am about to describe took place in 1938. Mr. and Mrs.
Coleman had a trailer caravan, and when they could get
away they would tour the country and, with proper, care-
free holiday independence, would stop for the night
wherever they felt inclined. On this occasion they were
returning from a tour in the West and were passing
through County Leitrim on their way back to Dublin. It
was August, and one fine evening, driving leisurely along
a country byroad and looking out for a convenient place
to stop, they eventually pulled up on the grass verge by
the gate of a rather swampy field which sloped gently
down towards a small stream where a supply of water
could be obtained.

Their caravan was very conveniently designed, and at
the rear they had fitted up a compartment as a kennel for
their two black cocker spaniels. They used to leave the
kennel door open so that the dogs could give warning of
any intruder venturing near during the night. The dogs
liked this post very much and used to sleep side by side,
their heads resting on the edge and their front paws
curved comfortably over it. From this position they were
all ears and eyes and noses on the alert, watchful of everything around them.

Mr. Coleman, as soon as they had settled on to the site,
took a bucket and went into the field in search of water,
while his wife busied herself getting things ready for the
night. It was about 10:00 o'clock and still quite light, and
the air was so still and quiet that one could almost feel
the stillness of it. As Mr. Coleman walked across the field,
his wife noticed an elderly woman, wearing the traditional
western shawl over her head, cross the field in the opposite

direction. She passed close to Mr. Coleman, then reached
and opened the gate. As she came near Mrs. Coleman she
turned and said in a very quiet and civil tone, "Good
evening!"

"Good evening," returned Mrs. Coleman.

"Are you stopping here tonight?" asked the woman, and
getting an affirmative reply, she added, "Then you ought
to leave something for the fairies," and with that she
quietly walked away.

If the strange woman had laughed and joked about it
or if she had been emphatic, Mrs. Coleman would have
looked upon it happily as a country joke or leg-pull, but
there was none of that at all. It was the quiet, matter-of-
fact casualness of the woman's way of speaking that was
so impressive. However, in the face of more practical prob-
lems of the house, Mrs. Coleman soon dismissed it from
her mind and set to work preparing the evening meal.
Later, just before turning in, she decided to put the butter
out in a cool place, as the weather was so warm. She had
bought a good supply that day, and now she took it all out
of the wrappers and put it into a bowl. There were two
or three pounds of it, and it filled the bowl completely;
she remembers well smoothing it across the top with a
knife, so as to level it with the brim. Then she took the
bowl out and put it on the road exactly under the compartment where the two dogs were already settled in for
the night. She placed an inverted plate over the bowl and
on top of the plate a heavy stone, so that it was secure
from the weather or from any minor raider. The bowl just
fitted in place, as there was only a clearance of a foot between the bottom of the compartment and the road.

The next morning, in the course of getting ready for

breakfast she went out to collect the butter and found the bowl safe and untouched, just as she had left it the night before. She took off the stone, threw it into the ditch, and carried the bowl and plate confidently into the caravan kitchen. But when she took off the plate she got a shock, for two thirds of the butter was gone, and in an astonishing way, too. All the butter had disappeared from one half of the bowl which was empty right to the bottom, as if one had cut down through the butter with a knife. The top part of the other half was also gone, having clearly been scraped out in a rounded way by something soft and blunt—a large tongue or a small hand, perhaps.

Who or what could have taken it, and how? That is the mystery which remains unsolved today. How could any human or any sizable animal get to the bowl without alarming the dogs? And if a human, whether grown up or child, had got to it, he would have taken the whole bowl. There was not room enough between the caravan floor and the ground for anyone to get the butter out *in situ,* and even if there had been, it must have been a noisy and lengthy process in the dark which could not have failed to arouse the dogs. No. A human, most emphatically, would have taken the bowl. Either he would have stolen both bowl and butter or he would have thrown the bowl away after removing the butter. And if he wanted the butter only, why take a part of it and not all? Above all, perhaps, why take the ridiculous and meaningless risk of replacing and recovering the bowl instead of throwing it into a ditch?

It is inconceivable that any human could have taken it, and no animal could possibly have replaced the plate and stone. By a simple process of elimination it inevitably comes down to the fairies, for from the old woman's words it was clearly a fairy country, and it looked it, too. Besides, this is just the sort of thing they do, traditionally.

THE POTATOES

This is an experience of nurse Mary Solon of Killeaden, and it took place some sixty years ago when she was a little girl of eight. Her father and mother were outstanding examples of old world character and virtue which one would rather expect to find in the pages of Jane Austen. They were prominent tenants on the Killeaden estate and were genuinely revered and respected by everyone in the place. Their cottage was a favorite resort of mine as a small boy when I escaped from the Big House and went wandering round the countryside. What a pleasant place it was for a youngster: always spotlessly clean both inside and outside in a way that is no mere figure of speech. I would get an unfailingly warm welcome and be set on a low three-legged milking stool by the open hearth, from which I could watch the potato-filled caldron bubbling and steaming as it hung from the crane over the glowing turf fire. I would be regaled with something that was sure to be tasty, perhaps a mug of lovely cool buttermilk or some slices of fresh soda bread (soda cake, we called it) with new rich butter melting on it, or maybe in the winter hot floury potato cakes which melted in one's mouth.

John Solon was a man to remember. He was tall, strongly built, and erect, and his heavy golden beard and whiskers framed a pair of wise, firm, but very kindly blue eyes. Throughout his family there was real discipline, which could on occasion be quite strictly enforced, as the little sally switch by the fireside showed. But all was done with such fairness, affection, and understanding that the whole family were models not only of good manners and punctilious truthfulness, but also of mutual affection, all of which survives to this day among that now elderly generation.

There were three John Solons on the estate, each with a large family, but all muddle was avoided by apt family descriptions added to their names. First, there was black-bearded and genial John Solon. He was the bailiff and was known as either "John Bailiff" or "Black John," and his family members as "Paddy Bailiff," "Mary Bailiff," and so on, or as "Paddy Black John," "Mary Black John," and so on. Next to him along the connecting bohereen which in its winding passage joined these little houses, were the Solons of whom I now write. This John Solon and nearly all his family had bright golden hair which graduated in some cases to light red. They were all known as the "Boy" Solons, "Boy" being the Anglicization of the Gaelic *Buidh,* pronounced "Bwee" and meaning yellow. Only two or three fields away came the "Red" John Solons who, as may be guessed, all had flaming red hair and the inevitable blue eyes. These three families were cousins, and good and friendly cousins too.

The incident which I am about to relate took place one evening towards the end of November when Anna-Maria Bailiff, Black John's eldest daughter, then a girl of eighteen or nineteen, was in the Boy Solons' house, having just looked in with some message and for the pleasure of a friendly chat. It transpired that the Boy Solons were rather short of milk, so Anna-Maria volunteered to go over to Red John Solon's with a jug and get some from him; his cow had recently calved, and for the moment he had

plenty and to spare. To keep her company she took little
Mary with her, and the child was delighted at the prospect
of such an evening outing. It was about eight o'clock and
fairly light still, as there was an early moon which was
nearly full, and the light clouds scurrying across the sky
served rather to emphasize the light than to dim it.

It was so lovely and light that on their way back they
left the little bridle path and took a short cut across two
small fields owned by a neighbor called Lavan. It was familiar ground to them, for all their lives they had known
and played over every foot of all the fields round about.
They had only a short walk before them, for the two cottages are not much more than about three hundred yards
apart by the path and perhaps some two hundred and
fifty or less by the fields.

Having filled the jug with milk, they duly started on
their homeward journey, Anna-Maria carrying the jug in
her right hand and holding Mary's hand with her left.
They proceeded quite normally across the first field and
climbed the loose stone wall at a low spot and got into the
second field. But as they crossed this field, Mary found
considerable difficulty in keeping up with her grown-up
companion, for it was a potato field with broad ridges
three feet wide and with foot-deep furrows in between.
The plants were in full growth, so that the ridges were
thick with tall green potato stalks matted together and
reaching well above her knees. It was not till afterwards
that she realized how extraordinary it was that these stalks
should still be green and fresh as late in the year as November, for by rights and in the normal cycle of nature
they should have withered and died down three months
or more before.

While Anna-Maria strode on easily, poor Mary found

it every moment harder and harder to keep up with her—
even to keep her feet—as she stumbled and jumped over
the difficult ground. And soon, to her grieved astonishment
her companion, instead of helping her over the worst
places, began to scold her for jumping about so and not
keeping quiet. But as the little girl continued to hop about,
her cousin's patience at last gave out.

"Now, if you don't walk quietly when I ask you, I will
tell your father when we get back, and you know he does
not like little girls to be so naughty. I've already spilt quite
a lot of the milk with the way you have upset me."

"But I can't help it," Mary replied in all earnestness.
"I must jump on to the ridges, and the potato stalks are
catching my legs all the time."

"Mary, it's the second time you've said that silly thing.
It is very naughty of you to go on pretending there are
potatoes when you know quite well there aren't."

"But, Anna-Maria, there *are*. Can't you *see* them?
Look, they are all round my legs now."

"Really, Mary, I have never before known you to be so
bad and bold and to tell such naughty stories. I will certainly tell your father when we get home."

And she shook the little girl and walked on full of indignation while Mary continued to jump and stumble as
before. What else could she do! In a few minutes, however, they came to the the bank and climbed over it out
of the field and then walked quietly home, but in silence,
as Anna-Maria was still too angry over what she thought
to be the wanton disobedience of a naughty girl.

So John Solon was duly told of his small daughter's
willful behavior, but in spite of everything she still persisted in asserting that it really was a potato field that they
had crossed and so she could not possibly get over it with-

out jumping and hopping. At this, her father was quick
to perceive that there was something queer in these con-
tradictory stories. Besides, he knew quite well that there
were not and never had been any potatoes in that particular field. He drew Mary to him, putting a hand on each
of her shoulders, and asked her to look him straight in the
eyes and tell him again that her account was really true.
Readily she assured him with all the emphasis she could
muster that every single thing she had said was true. As
he looked into her honest and innocent eyes, he had no
hesitation in believing that she was entirely sincere in all
she said.

So he sent her off to bed with a kiss and a kindly word
and then turned to Anna-Maria to explain the solution
which had occurred to him. The next morning after breakfast he raised the matter again, and again Mary repeated
her story word for word the same as the evening before.
So then he took her by the hand and led her out to the
field in question. Lifting her over the bank, he walked
with her all over it, examining it fully in the clear light
of day. And there it was, under her feet as she walked,
just an ordinary field of grazing grass which had not
grown a crop of any kind for many years. She was astonished to see it so, and yet in another way she was not, for
now she remembered quite well that the field never had
been potatoes as long as she could think back. Yet it certainly was so the night before, and she still had no doubt
on that score nor has she ever since to this very day, for
after all these years the memory of that extraordinary
night is still quite vivid in her mind, and she can see those
tangled potato stalks and the ridges and furrows as well
as she did that night.

What was the meaning of it all, one may well ask.

Surely the answer is, just nothing. Only a prank played by some fairies upon a little girl who happened to be attuned to the occult. It was mischievous, perhaps, but all the same quite harmless and friendly, more to be laughed at than to get angry about, which anyway is a futile thing to do when one is faced with the earth folk. These things happen often in the country, much more often than "superior" people realize—and may they long continue.

THE FARMER AND THE FAIRIES

Mickey O'Mahoney has a tidy farm of some fifteen acres, and his nice thatched one-story house of the old traditional kind lies on the very shore of a large lough in County Mayo. Unless one rows over in a boat, it is only to be reached by going to the end of a long bohereen or narrow high-banked lane which runs from the nearest road. This lane ends at his yard, which slopes sharply down from it till, about ten feet lower, it reaches a high protective stone wall built on the edge of the pebbly shore of the lough. In a strong easterly wind or when the lough is swollen after a period of heavy rains, it is easily seen how vital a necessity that wall is.

Mickey, who is a particular friend of mine, is a sturdy bachelor living by himself except for the companionship of his dog and farm animals, which are his constant care. Altogether he is a fine type of countryman and one that any race can be proud of, for he is essentially honest, intelligent and self-reliant. It is always a joy to me to sit by his open hearth, with its strong, finely made crane holding a bubbling pot over the warm and glowing turf fire. The crane's history is known. It was made by a local smith about 120 years ago, and it is a privilege for anyone who appreciates

good artisanship to look at it closely and note the excellent
and sturdy way in which each piece has been either welded
or jointed together.

The little lane, before it reaches Mickey's yard, serves
nearly a dozen other cottages in its course; the nearest
must be some 200 to 300 yards away. The last five or six
houses are all dependent on the same spring, which
bubbles up out of the ground in the middle of a small field
in the next farm to Mickey's. It is a curious spring for it is,
as it were, so sudden. One can walk across the field without any suspicion of this sheer hole in the ground until one
is right on top of it, when there it is, about two feet deep
and five feet across and overhung by the cropped-grass-
covered clay on all sides. It is a limpid pool of clear water
which one can watch bubbling up out of the virgin rocks
that form its sides and bottom. It runs off merrily down to
the lough in a little rill which is just as sheer and is hardly
a foot and a half wide. There is a large flagstone to step
down onto which is only three inches above the surface of
the pool, and the rill gurgles rapidly round one end of it in
a miniature cascade. Of course, just behind this flagstone
and overshadowing it there is the inevitable gnarled and
ancient thorn tree, so beloved of the fairies.

The water is delicious. I have often lapped it up from
my cupped hands on a warm summer's day, but it is hard
water as well as cool, for it comes through limestone from
goodness knows how far away.

One night in October 1957 Mickey's cow was calving,
which is always an important economic event to a man in
his position. Good and conscientious farmer that he is, he
stayed with the animal till the little newcomer had safely
arrived and mother and youngster had been tended and
comfortably bedded down.

Back in his own house, he saw it was already after two in the morning, and he was tired and felt an urgent desire for a large cup of hot, strong, and sweet tea. So, instead of turning in, he stirred up the fire, raking away the ashes so carefully piled up over the glowing embers, added more sods of turf, and with the help of the bellows soon had a fine warm fire lighting up the hearth. But when he went to fill the kettle and hang it on the crane he found that the water bucket was quite empty. That did not bother him much, however, for the night was fine and it would be a pleasant stroll along to the spring. So he set off happily with his bucket in one hand and his hurricane lantern in the other, leaving his dog to mind the house while he was away.

The night was not too dark, for though there was no moon there were plenty of stars and no clouds to hide them, and his lantern was rather a convenience than a necessity. He walked up the lane to the clumsy stone steps which were set in the high bank as a rough stile, climbed over them into the field, and went straight to the spring. When he arrived, he stepped down onto the flagstone, placed the lantern on it beside him and, using both hands, dipped the bucket into the pool and drew it out nearly full. Holding the pail in his left hand, he bent down to pick up the lantern, but just as his hand had reached it, it was suddenly kicked—or knocked—from under his hand into the pool. He made a quick grab at it and was lucky enough just to catch it before the glass hit the water.

Parts of it were too hot to hold, so he had to drop it quickly on the flagstone. He put the bucket down and attended to the lantern, seeing that nothing was damaged and turning the wick up a little. It had all been so sudden and unexpected, the "kick" and the recovery, that he did not stop just then to think *why* it had happened. His concern at the moment was merely that it *had* happened.

When he turned to take up the bucket, he discovered that in the effort of saving the lamp he had spilled most of his water, so, leaving the lantern on the flagstone, he again dipped his bucket into the pool. As before, he filled it nearly full, and as before he changed the bucket from both hands to his left and stretched out his right to take up the lantern again. But before he could touch it, it got an even more violent kick, which shot it right into the pool. He had no chance of saving it, and as it sank down the cold water shattered the hot glass into innumerable pieces and, what was worse, the lantern proceeded to ooze out its oil, polluting all the water so that it was made quite unusable.

Mickey stood staring in amazement, and the impossibility of the "kicks" having any natural or normal cause sank inescapably into his mind. As he stood there musing on this, a low mischievous chuckle came from almost beside him in the field. He looked towards the sound and across the empty field with indignation. "Oh, ye rascals," he muttered, "Sure, you're the divils for tricks." With that he stripped off his coat, rolled up his right sleeve and, plunging his arm into the pool, recovered his damaged lantern. In doing so, he was careful not to let his coat out of his other hand, for he was taking no risks of further pranks, very wisely. Then, putting the lamp between his feet, he slipped his coat on again, wet arm and all, took the bucket in his left hand and the lamp in his right and started off for the stile. He had not got halfway to it when he heard another chuckle behind him. He swung round and gazed into the empty spaces, and then in final indignation he said defiantly, "I wish to glory I could catch ye, for

tis the switch you want and no mistake and gladly and
soundly I'd give it ye."

Having thus relieved his feelings he strode off for home
and was soon swallowing a large mug of strong, steaming
hot tea with plenty of sugar. This eased his feelings a lot,
though by the time he was ready to turn into bed it was
after four o'clock in the morning. Tired as he was, he found
he could not sleep, for the pangs of conscience began to attack him—quite unfairly, I have always thought, but then
"conscience" is, in my own experience, a most unfair companion.

He was worried at the thought of his unfortunate
neighbors, some with large families of small children who,
when they went to draw lovely fresh water for the day's
cooking, would find it contaminated with paraffin oil and
their tea ruined and perhaps their food, too. In the end,
conscience, that persistent bully, won, and as a result, at
about seven in the morning, an hour after dawn, he wearily
got up, took another bucket and a cloth, and returned to
the spring. He set to work with vigor and baled the pool till
it was quite dry. Then he carefully cleared up all the
broken glass into a paper and thoroughly rubbed down the
rocks with his cloth, working steadily till he was sure it was
free of oil. He stood back and watched the fresh water
bubble up once more till the pool was nearly half full,
when he tasted the water to make certain all was well
again. Assured on that point, he went home and did his
best to make up for his lost rest.

He wisely let a number of months pass before he mentioned the incident, and then only to reliable friends. He
was waiting till it would be too late for anyone to imagine
oil when there was none. He does not bear the slightest ill

will to the local "little people," but feels it to be rather a sign of their affection. "Sure, isn't it in their nature," he will say philosophically, but all the same I am sure he would rather they played their pranks on his neighbors in future and left him alone.

THE CANVAS

In 1947, we in Ireland were still suffering from the austerities and deprivations of the war, and cars were one of those amenities of modern life which had not yet returned to general use. Early in June of that year an artist friend of mine, Miss E. M., was staying in Connemara while she painted a number of landscapes of that windswept but beautiful country. With this purpose in view she one day deposited her bicycle, her painting equipment, and herself on to a bus plying from Roundstone to Ma'am Cross. Before reaching Ma'am Cross she had herself put down at an isolated point some three miles to the west of that place. There she left the high road and cycled along narrow cart tracks, keeping all the time a critical eye on the countryside.

She had not gone more than a couple of miles before she saw just the spot she was looking for. It was a low hillock some fifty yards or so from the track, and from it she felt sure she could overlook a particularly attractive stretch of country. Before starting she had loaded her cycle with all the things she thought she might want, and to a hypercritical eye she might have looked a little like the White Knight in *Through the Looking Glass,* for her easel was strapped to the frame of her cycle, her box of paints and brushes and such things were piled in the basket on the handlebars, while her stool, waterproof, and

The Killeaden thorn, an important fairy tree which the author's grandfather moved from the fairy fort Lis Ard to this site in front of his house. He subsequently lost heavily in stock and money. *(See pages 49, 50.)*

A fairy fort which from time to time is seen blazing with lights after dark. Generations
people have seen this fairy activity taking place. *(See page 136.)*

The famous fairy fort of Lis Ard, of which the blind poet Raftery sang. It has been se
crowded with fairy folk, life-sized, the women mostly young and good looking, the men we
ing brown or red coats and conical hats. *(See page 38.)*

An oak at the foot of Lis Ard under which fairies dance and hold meetings at certain times of the year. *(See page 51.)*

The demon thorn tree. In reality it is three trees—two thorns and a bourtree. It is guarded by three malevolent demons, and there are tales of passers-by late at night who have had their arms fiercely gripped or who have heard blood-chilling laughs and angry spittings. *(See page 52.)*

Paddy Baine's house. The original corner was removed when it was found to be standing on a fairy path. Its removal brought an end to the serious disturbances which the fairies were causing. *(See page 127.)*

The river Gweestion, where boys poach salmon. A would-be poacher once failed to appear at a river rendezvous and later was found nearby, lost and with no idea of his whereabouts. He had been a victim of the "stray sod," a spell by which the fairies cause persons to lose their bearings in places familiar to them. *(See page 156.)*

The fairy trilogy of oak, ash, and thorn (center, right, and left). By the light of a waxing moon one gathers a twig of each and binds the ends with threads of bright scarlet wool as protection against hostile spirits. *(See page 51.)*

The road of the three dark figures. Here, two men walking home saw three weird figures in black, facing each other in a tight triangle. The men hurried past, but the same figures reappeared farther on, having been transported with magical swiftness. *(See pages 36, 37.)*

The Big House. In a room entered by the rightmost of the two doors lived Biddy Cosgary (Mrs. Groak). There, with the help of a mouthful of water from the magic well in the background, Biddy caused troublesome objects to disappear from visitors' eyes. *(See page 87.)*

(*Left to right*) Martin Groak, son of Biddy Cosgary and coachman for the Mac Manus famil
the author's aunts, Miss Lottie Mac Manus, novelist, and Miss Emma Mac Manus, who inte
viewed Biddy Cosgary; Mrs. C. E. Mac Manus, the author's grandmother; Mrs. Mac Manus
granddaughter. (*See pages 86, 87.*)

other necessities, including a picnic lunch, were on the rear carrier. As convenience was much more important than appearance in that lonely region, her large canvas, 24 by 20 inches, was hung from her shoulders like the rear board of a sandwichman.

As soon as she had decided on this spot, she dismounted and began busily to unpack the things she needed, laying her machine on the grass verge. There was only a small, shallow ditch between the track and the rolling unfenced country beyond, and it was easily negotiated, a long step being quite sufficient to take one across. After that, it was an easy walk of a few perches to the grassy hillock she had in view. Taking her canvas with her, she started off and soon found the place she wanted, which was about half way up the little slope. She put her canvas down to mark the site, carefully placing its clean white surface uppermost. Owing to the slope of the hill it lay at an angle of 30°, facing toward the road.

She set off to collect the rest of her things, but before

stepping over the ditch again she turned round to look
back at the canvas and to renew her approval of the site
she had chosen. There lay the canvas, stretched taut on
its frame and positively scintillating, its virgin whiteness
emphasized by the bright summer sunshine and by its
background of short, coarse green grass. Satisfied, she
strode on to the road and, her hands full with bundles,
turned to the ditch. She looked up casually to get her bearings from the canvas, but no canvas was to be seen. She
stood stock still with astonishment while she searched the
ground, but the more she looked the less she saw that
looked like her precious canvas. The short grass stretched
before her everywhere, with neither crack nor cranny
where anything could hide. There was no wind to blow it
away, nor was there either human or animal anywhere in
sight that could have moved it.

Quite sure that she must have made some absurd mistake, Miss E. M. walked quickly up to the hillock and put
her things down at the spot where she imagined she had
left her canvas. She then began a thorough and systematic
search for it, quartering the ground in every direction. But
it was all in vain. She could see clearly in every direction
and not even a small or dull-colored object could escape
her eye, certainly not anything as large and bright as her
canvas. After some time, she went to the top of the hillock
to have a final look round, but again it was useless, and
she stood there baffled and understandably irritated at the
fantastic situation.

The more she looked about her, the more bewildered
she became. It did not make sense, yet there was no getting away from the essential fact that there was no canvas
there, nor anywhere else for that matter. Miss E. M. is an
intelligent, sensible girl with a well-balanced mind, and it

was the outrage to all logic and common sense which irritated her as much as the waste of her time and energies.
However, there clearly was nothing she could do about it,
so after some time she reluctantly retraced her steps, went
to her cycle, spread her waterproof sheet on the grass
verge, and settled down on it to eat her lunch and smoke
a cigarette at comfortable leisure. She still had a couple of
hours to pass till she should collect her things and pack
before making her way back to the main road in time for
the returning bus.

Half an hour later, lying at ease and looking up at the
deep blue of the summer sky, she idly turned over on her
side to gaze at the little hill. The next moment, her cigarette thrown aside, she was sitting up and staring with
open-mouthed astonishment at her canvas, its white surface shining as brightly as ever in the sunlight. It was
lying straight in front of her and in the exact spot where
she had originally left it. The affair was now becoming
eerie rather than irritating, so she got up and quite warily
began to make her way back to the hillock.

Though by this time the afternoon was advanced and
the shadows were lengthening, it was still broad daylight
and everything was just as clear as when she first dismounted from her cycle. In a few moments she was standing on the hillside looking down at the delinquent canvas,
which lay just where she had left it and within six feet
of the equipment she had placed there. Rather gingerly
she picked it up and examined it all over, back and front,
with great care. But it bore no sign of any adventure or
of any kind of movement, neither scratch nor mark nor
stain. It was, she had to admit, just as clean and neat and
well behaved as ever. By now the sun was low in the sky
and it was too late to get any painting done, so it only re-

mained to go back to the road and pack. She put the canvas under her arm and started off, but she had not gone a dozen steps when she stopped short. She had had one lesson and did not want another: to leave her other things untended was just asking for a second and probably an even more annoying one. So she turned with a weary sigh and retraced her steps to the other things, hung her canvas over her shoulder once more and, filling her arms with bundles, made quite sure of getting all her precious belongings safely back to the road.

There she packed, mounted her cycle, and made her way back to the bus route on the high road. Having some time to wait, she rode along till she came to a snugly thatched white cottage close to the road. She dismounted and went in to chat for a few moments and enquire for certain about her bus. The woman of the house received her with all the friendly ease of the western country woman, and when Miss E. M. recounted her adventure, she laughed gently but with full understanding. "Ah!" she remarked. "What else would you expect now? Sure, isn't that a fairy hill!"

Then the bus was sighted and, hailing it, my friend returned to her rooms with much food for quiet thought.

FAIRY WIND

The fairy wind is a curious phenomenon. It seems to me to be much the same as those queer "Dust Devils" which one sees in the East. There, during the hot weather in dry sandy districts, little whirlwinds are started which draw the dust up into the air in rapidly twirling spirals that move across the country at varying speeds and sometimes assume fantastic shapes. These weird columns of dust can on occasion widen out at the top till they look like gigantic figures with outstretched, menacing arms. It is with relief that at length one sees them sink down again and disappear into the ground. In the dry Deccan plateau in India I have seen as many as twenty at one time, of sizes varying from ten to sixty feet in height and moving in different directions. Some were quite terrifying to look at and could not fail to make people think of giants and genies.

An Irish variant of this phenomenon took place as recently as 1955, when Mrs. V. Fitzgerald of Turlough Park, near Castlebar, walked out one afternoon to her big walled garden. This garden is some way from the house, and to reach it one must cross a large field with the romantic name of Gortnafullagh—in English, the Field of Blood. We are rather fond of calling places after some gory incident of the past, and I know a number of fields with the same kind of name. This field was a meadow that year and it had not long been mown. The hay was made up into what we in Ireland call "lapcocks," little bundles of fairly loose hay about the size of a large drawing-room pouffe. The air was very hot and still that afternoon, and a heat haze dimmed the more distant trees.

As Mrs. Fitzgerald strolled leisurely along, she suddenly saw to her amazement a number of the little lapcocks rise into the air for about ten feet and, whirling rapidly, sail gaily away for fifty yards or more over a fence, disappearing into the next field. As the little cocks rotated, they rapidly disintegrated into loose wisps of hay. But there seemed no reason for these startling antics, as the air was utterly still, with not even the suggestion of a breeze. Actually these whirlwinds can take place only when there is no general lateral movement of air at all, and even when quite close to them one feels no breeze.

This phenomenon, which can occur suddenly in the quiet Irish countryside, is so rare and so startling that it is easy for it to be identified with fairies and suchlike. It would be amazing if it were not, and in India the "Dust Devils" are ascribed to genies. The two unquestionably are blood brothers and arise from exactly the same physical laws. But while accepting this natural explanation, one should not blindly attempt to explain all unusual movements on the same lines, for some are much more difficult to assess when looked into closely. Here is a case in point.

I remember a curious occurrence that took place in County Longford, a few years before the war. A group of six or seven people—men, women, and a couple of youngsters—were busy making hay in a long, narrow field, one end of which was high and the other a good deal lower. It was the first time this field had been made a meadow and now, having made the hay, they were busy saving it into fairly large compact cocks six feet high or more. On the high part of the field they had found a large flat rock, only a few inches higher than the grass, which formed an ideal dry and firm base on which to build one of the cocks.

An hour or two later, as they were working in the lower end of the field, one of the children cried out a warning. They looked up quickly, to see the cock which they had made on the rock rise a few feet into the air, move half a dozen yards to one side, and settle down safely on to the grass again in its new place. They stared with astonishment and then went up to investigate more closely. Sure enough, there was the cock standing safely on the grass, with the hay ropes across it as taut as ever. Not even a wisp of hay was left on the rock. They wisely

left it there, feeling that the rock was clearly appointed
to other fairy uses and was not to be interfered with. It
is difficult to see how this can be accounted for by any
ordinary whirlwind.

Fairy Music and Dancing

About 1904 young Johnnie S., who was then em-
ployed by my grandmother, was busy in the orchard one
summer afternoon. It was about 3:00 p.m., and as he was
scything nettles near the stables the sound of music and
dancing floated down to him through the trees from the
old garden house that stood on a rise at the further end.
This puzzled him, as the garden house was semi-derelict
at that time. It had only two rooms, one above the other,
and its door and windows had gone. The stairs had vanished, except for the first four or five steps, which were of
stone, though the roof and the upper floor were sound
enough. I can remember it as it was then, for, a few years
later, just before it was repaired, I used the upstairs room
as a pirate lair or bandits' cave. I kept all sorts of treasures
there, a home-made bow and arrows and a very special
catapult fork of holly which I had cut for myself in great
Drummin wood on the shores of Lough Cullen. Standing
on the top stone step, a boy could just peep into the upper
room, and it was not too difficult with the agility of youth
to climb up into it with the precarious help of projecting
stones on each side. A friendly barn owl used to live somewhere in the rafters, and the way it would silently swish
through the little windows, in the twilight, with apparent
ease in spite of its great wing span, was a constant cause
of wonder to me.

Hearing the music, Johnnie came to the conclusion

that some lads of the village were having a gay time when
all good people should be at work; what was worse, they
had the effrontery to do it under the nose of the Big
House. This state of affairs obviously required instant in-
vestigation. As he walked up through the trees, the noise
of the music and the stamping of dancing feet became
louder, and he could hear the gay laughter and talk mixed
up with it. But when he got quite close to the house, the
music suddenly ceased and an utter silence fell on the
place. He now knew he had caught them, for they had no
way of escape, so he entered the doorway, ran up the few
steps, and swung himself quickly into the upper room—
to find it absolutely empty. There was no place for even a
mouse to hide, and no one could have escaped through
the tiny windows.

Johnnie's nerves now thoroughly shaken, he hastily
beat a retreat, and as he went down the stone steps he
looked out through the empty door to Lis Ard, the great
fairy fort less than a quarter of a mile away, and then he
knew. Besides, he had not gone twenty paces from the little house when the music, the dancing, and the laughter
of a happy crowd started again, now even louder than
ever as if in derision. So he returned forthwith to the stables, deciding that the nettles in the orchard could well
wait till another day.

Johnnie is alive and flourishing today, and he remembers well this curious incident.

Fairy Ground and Paths

For all the hillside was haunted
By the faery folk come again;
And down in the heart-light enchanted
Were opal-coloured men.

AE

                             Ireland is closely dotted with places sacred to the fairies, and place names show how ancient is their claim to some of these sites. Small hills and hillocks are their favored haunts, but because many of these same hillocks were also convenient situations for the stockaded houses or groups of houses of the ancient Irish, the two sets of people are as often as not mistakenly muddled up together. But the fairy preference is by no means confined to these raths, duns, and lisses, for they often adopt patches of rough ground or small boulder-strewn glens and untamed clumps of trees. It is

123

usually in these special haunts of theirs, in hills and fields and glens, that they are sometimes seen, busy at their community affairs. They visit continuously from one place to another and usually along some well-used fairy pass which is quite invisible to human eyes, but woe to the human who builds across it and thus obstructs their freedom of movement.

All this is quite accepted by the Irish country people as a normal part of life. In 1932, when I lived in Longford, an old woman told my authoress aunt how, when she was a girl of eighteen and worked as a maid at the Big House, one summer's day on her afternoon off she and some other girls were sitting by a lough not far from the avenue gates when they heard the clatter of horsemen coming along the road. She jumped up at once, saying she must hurry back to the house, as there was "quality" coming and her help would be needed.

She had not run far when the party of riders came in sight, eight of them, men and young women, in bright clothes and with colored bridles and saddles, the girls aside, the men astride, and all laughing and talking gaily. They were no more than forty yards from her when they swung to the right over a grassy bank, across a small field, and into the side of a small thorn-ringed fairy fort. Horses and all, they trotted into the earth as coolly and casually as humans would pass through a stable gate. So she shrugged her shoulders and went back to her companions. When asked why she had returned, she replied, "Ah, 'twas no quality, at all. 'Twas only a pack of fairies going into the fort." What struck my aunt, who was highly experienced in these matters, and myself was the obviously genuine unaffectedness of her acceptance of fairies as an everyday fact, and no matter at all for wonder or worry.

Horseback, fairy or otherwise, is by no means their only method of traveling. Short distances, of course, they do on foot, but when going longer excursions they are reputed to use frequently the buachalan bui or yellow ragwort. So if you come across a ragwort that has been pulled up by the roots and thrown carelessly on the grass, you may suspect that a fairy has been riding it, especially if the plant is a tall, strong one. The fairies use ragwort, it is said, as witches use their brooms, and since our Irish countryside is heavily infested with this pretty weed, our fairy friends must find it a great convenience. I suppose they must disapprove of the good husbandman who keeps his land clean of weeds.

There is cause for worry if their rights or their paths are interfered with. Here are two stories which I have known all my life, for they concern people who live only a few miles from my home. I give these accounts word for word as they were sent to me recently by a friend in whose accuracy and integrity I place the highest reliance.

Mickey Langan's Frustrated House Building

Mickey Langan grew so tired of trespassing hens, ducks, and geese (his own as much as those of neighbors) that he decided to move his own residence to the outskirts of the village where he had a piece of land named Pairc Rua.

Without a word to anybody, Mickey set out very early one morning and on arrival at Pairc Rua he quickly selected the new site on a small hill. The view towards Mount Nephin and a spur of the Ox Mountains was lovely. Near the spot flowed a brook, and a short distance away was an ancient spring. The nearest neighbor was at least

a quarter of a mile away. There would be no more trouble
about hens, ducks, and geese. Carefully, he looked at a
few fairy forts. He was not in a direct line between any
two of them, and therefore his new home would in no way
hinder the progress of the fairy hosts as they swept back
and forth on their nightly expeditions.

All seemed well. Mickey put up some markers for the
foundations of his new house, sprinkled a little holy water
on the spot, and proceeded to dig the foundations. After
a few hours a neighbor came along the road and shouted,
"Bail O Dia ort, ae cad. Ta Tu a deanam, a Micael?"
Mickey told him what he was doing, but the neighbor
warned him that he feared that place might not be suitable. Why did he not consult the wise woman, Mairead
ni Heine, who lived near Swinford? Mickey, being of a
somewhat peppery temper, simply snorted and went on
with his work. "Throth," he muttered to himself, "you,
Tom Walsh, are never lost for an excuse to stop work!"

Tom must have spread the news, however. Soon Mickey's wife, Kitty, appeared with some breakfast, which
gave her an excuse for coming. "Misha, Mickey, aghra,
what are you doing?" Mickey informed her and was again
warned of the necessity of consulting Mairead ni Heine. In
the course of the morning there were several visitors, all
with the same unsolicited advice. When he came home for
dinner he found Kitty surrounded by several old cronies.
She was in tears, poor soul. This was more than Mickey
could stand. He got his old mule and set off for Corra na
Coll to arrange for a visit from Mairead. The good lady
promised an early visit, and true to her word she soon
came. One glance at the site and Mairead uttered a definite
condemnation. "Not here, Mickey, not here," she said. And
that was the end of poor Mickey's cherished plan.

ALTERATION IN PADDY BAINE'S HOUSE

Paddy Baine had built his house without consultation with anybody, wise or otherwise. Shortly after he and his bride, Biddy Callan, took up residence in the new house, they began to experience very frequent disturbances at one end of it which abutted on the little village road. Some nights it appeared as if the whole house was about to tumble down. Paddy consulted his parents and also the parents of his wife. The upshot of a conference of the two sets of parents was that Paddy, acting on their advice, went to Corra na Coll to call Mairead ni Heine. In due time she came and after an inspection of the house she declared that a corner of the house, one of those abutting on the road, must be removed. It was interfering with the progress of the "good people." Paddy at once called in Paddy Kielty, the local stonemason, and very soon one corner of the house was cut across. The house is still occupied by Paddy's descendants, but there has been no return of the old disturbances. It is known that occasionally through the years a sudden fierce gust of wind would blow around this corner, even in the calmest weather.

It may be of some significance that Paddy Baine's house was the nearest to the ill-fated site Mickey Langan had chosen some years before.

But wise people are not so impetuous as Mickey Langan and Paddy Baine, for the usual practice, if there is the least doubt about fairy approval, is to turn one sod on the site in the evening and leave it overnight. If in the morning it is found turned back again, then the fairies disapprove and some other site must be found. If, however, the sod is untouched, then it is all right and work can go ahead at once.

BUILDING TO THE WEST

A point that must always be remembered is that on no account should a house be extended in a westerly direction unless it is into a space already artificially enclosed, such as a garden or a yard. To extend a house into a field or any open ground or across a path lying to the west is fatal. Here is a typical case, but as I have not yet succeeded in checking all the details and as, anyway, it is too poignant, I shall not give the place or names of the people concerned.

About the year 1935, Dr. "O'Kelly" of Ballyblank had a curious series of cases. He had been called in by Michael O'Hagan, a man living in a good type of country cottage not far outside the town. His eldest son was ill but, examine him as he might, Dr. O'Kelly could not find what was wrong with him. The lad got worse and worse till, after a couple of weeks, he died. Then the man's next child was taken ill with the same mysterious complaint, but although Dr. O'Kelly called in a second opinion, it was of no avail and this child also died. Then the next child sickened and the same tragic course was run. Soon after that the fourth child was also taken, and all the doctors were still completely baffled.

Finally, his fifth child, a boy of six or seven, was in his turn taken ill in the same way and he sickened desperately. After seeing him one evening the doctor was satisfied that he was in an even worse state than any of the others had been and was certain to die during the night.

Dr. O'Kelly lived in a substantial house in the town with a big front garden. As he was completing his dressing the next morning he saw Michael O'Hagan coming up to the house. He hurried down to meet him, knowing he would hear of the poor child's death, but to his amazement the news was exactly the opposite. "Doctor, you needn't come any more. The boy is well and there'll be no more deaths." This astounding statement demanded an explanation and the doctor got it.

It seems that, as soon as he had left the evening before, the distraught father, seeing the utter failure of official medicine to save his children, had gone off to a wise woman, the successor of the famous Mairead ni Heine, who had come to his house immediately. She saw the cause of all the trouble at first glance. Some months before all these illnesses had begun, Michael O'Hagan had built an additional room as an extension to his house, but in doing so he had made two fatal mistakes. In the first place, the extension was to the west and was built on to the western gable of his house. What was worse, it was built into an open field and not into a garden or enclosed space.

In the second place, this extension just obtruded into a straight line between two neighboring fairy forts. The wise woman told him that as soon as he had demolished this extension his child would get well, but that if he failed to do so it would die the next day and his sixth and last child would inevitably die after it.

So Michael O'Hagan set to work at once with a pick-axe, toiling steadily through the night. He finished his work as dawn was breaking, and when he went into his house he found with joy that his little son had sunk into a deep and healthy sleep and the color was already returning to its cheeks. A few hours later it awoke refreshed and well, though still weak and debilitated. With joy in his heart the happy father went up to the doctor's house with his glad news.

Now, this story is not at all dependent on the doctor's uncorroborated account, for all the neighbors knew of it, they had been at the funerals, and had seen the extension to the house demolished and the little boy running about again, fully recovered.

DANCING LIGHTS

Between Kiltimagh and Bohola in County Mayo there is a crossroad called Shanaghy, where the boys and girls of the neighborhood used to gather of an evening to listen to the tales of some wandering storyteller, or shanachie, or to dance to the lively tunes of a "musicianer." The westward road at this cross wanders over a wild country till it reaches the slopes of Slieve Cairn, a long, narrow, isolated hill running north and south and rising sharply out of the surrounding plain. In the flank of this hill there is a gorge, known as the Cliff, slashed deeply into it, its

steep sides covered with lush bilberries. A sparkling
stream rushes turbulently along the bottom. It is a lovely
spot and was a favorite place for summer picnics when we
were young. All this area from hill to crossroads is extremely rich in fairy folklore; tales abound, concerning
recent times as well as olden days.

One spot in particular is locally reputed to be strictly
appropriated to the use of the fairy clans of the earth folk,
and to have been so from time immemorial. It is a very
curious-looking, rough patch of ground, for no ditch or
bank divides it from the road, an unusual thing in Ireland,
while to a depth of fifteen or twenty yards inwards the
ground is covered by strange little grass mounds, for all
the world the shape of lapcocks of hay or of large pouffes
in a lady's boudoir, and lying some three feet apart. Behind them is a mass of rushes interspersed with more
mounds, but not nearly so thickly, and this continues to
the bank of the next field.

Stories are still told of how, whenever in the past anyone was foolish or avaricious enough to try to enclose this
bit of land, he would find the next morning that his fences
or banks had been thrown down and his ditches filled up
during the night by some mysterious agency. This would
often be followed by minor household or farm troubles
and disorders, sufficient to indicate clearly the displeasure
of the fairies and to serve as a warning to keep clear of
such trespass on their rights in future. This ground lies
only about a quarter of a mile from the crossroads on the
way to the Cliff and is on the right or northern side of the
road where it forks for the first time.

When I was a small boy of six or seven, the whole
of our family, with the addition of some of my mother's
relations who were down from Dublin, went out to the

Cliff one hot, sunny summer's day for a big picnic, bringing with us plentiful provisions for lunch and tea. We
had, I think, a wagonette and pair of horses as well as two
jaunting cars. These were the old Irish open, single-horse
car with swinging side seats which could be folded up
when not in use. We children had a lovely day of fun and
activity, and the gloaming had already begun by the time
everything had been cleared up and stowed on to the ve-
hicles and we had started on our five-mile homeward
journey. How we sorted ourselves out I do not know, but
I found myself with my mother on the left side of one of
the jaunting cars, with some elderly relative on the other
side. Bundles of picnic hamper were piled in the middle,
and the driver sat in front, perched close above his horse's
quarters. I was a tired little boy, nestling under the rug
close up against my mother's skirts. I was not really
asleep but only half dozing when I was awakened completely by an exclamation of delighted surprise from my
mother, who cried out, "Oh, look at the pretty lights!" This
was immediately followed by a burst of expletives from
the driver, accompanied by furious lashes of his whip on
the startled horse, which then plunged forward from its
easygoing amble into a wild gallop. We all frantically
hung on for dear life to the swaying and jerking car. My
mother with some difficulty managed to secure both herself and me and at last persuaded the driver to slow down
to a safer pace, when she demanded to know what was
the matter with him. I do not remember any more, for I
was soon sound asleep and hardly noticed being undressed
and put to bed later, but I have often heard discussed all
that happened.

It appears that my mother saw this patch of ground
covered with what seemed to her to be hundreds, but were

probably only dozens, of little twinkling lights rather like fireflies. Most of them were about a foot or a little more off the ground and moved around with occasional bobbing up and down. They were all the same color, a pale yellow, and sparkled in the prettiest way up and down over the mounds and in and out through the rushes. That they could be anything having to do with the fairies never occurred to her for a moment till the driver declared that it was the "Shee" out and about, and "The Lord protect us from them!" Why he was so frightened, it is difficult to understand, and it is curious that he merely had a glimpse of the lights and then only when his attention had been drawn to them by my mother's exclamation. But I saw them, too, and to this day I can still conjure up in my mind those little twinkling lights which I glimpsed as I woke up with the cries of the driver, the protests of my mother, and the imminent fear of being thrown off the swaying car.

What can the explanation of these things be? Whatever else it may be, it is neither imagination nor invention. The lights could be neither fireflies nor glowworms, I am quite sure of that. As far as I know, these kinds of insects do not exist in Ireland. Apart from that, I have since lived for years in a country full of fireflies and they could not be mistaken for those lights. Fireflies move quickly, as any flying insect does, dodging here and there and up and down in quite a different way, while glowworms do not move at all, let alone glide gently through the air.

Two years ago, when staying with my brother, someone recalled this incident to my mind and I determined to have another look at that romantic little piece of ground, for I had not even thought of it for many years. About 3:00 o'clock on a warm and drowsy Sunday afternoon I bor-

rowed his car and drove out there. Having turned at the
crossroads, I was soon approaching the place when I saw
to my surprise that it and the fields all round it were almost literally black with crows and daws. Only a com-
paratively few circled overhead, and the noise of their
cawing became quite deafening as I got nearer, far above
the noise of my engine. But when I reached the nearest of
the birds, their behavior became curious. The cawing
stopped at once and there was solid silence, which hit the
ear even more than their previous raucous cawing. Added
to that, instead of taking to the air as they normally would,
they all remained on the ground and merely hopped out
of the way of the car. Going very slowly, lest I run over
one of them, I turned the car at the fork and got out. I
walked over to the nearest of the little hummocks. But
still the birds stayed on the ground, keeping their distance
from me and with their little beady eyes turned towards
me, while maintaining an utter silence that began to feel
positively eerie.

However, I was not going to be put off my exploration
by any flock of birds, so, after ineffectually clapping my
hands and shooing at them, I stepped off the road and began to examine the little mounds. I had not gone far when
I came across one mound which some cattle must have
trodden upon. A lump was torn away at the top, leaving
a little flat ledge of curious red-brown earth. And in the
middle of this ledge lay a small jet-black stone of the
shape and size of an ordinary matchbox.

Now, in folk tales all over this countryside, time and
again a black stone, generally a small one, plays an important role, in witchcraft particularly but also in fairy
lore, and to such an extent that one would think they were
fairly common. But they seem to be quite rare, and I have

for some years kept my eyes open for one during my frequent rambles, but without success. I have found a number of stones that were very dark blue or gray, but never a truly black one as is coal. Yet here, in this reputedly fairy ground, I find one ready laid out for me. It is before me now as I write, for I picked it up and put it in my pocket as a curio.

There was not much to see, apart from the curiously shaped mounds and their red earth, so after a few minutes I walked back toward the car. The whole way, I was the hub of an empty circle in a black sea of birds, which were never more than ten paces away and which quietly fell back before me and closed in behind me as I moved. I felt no sense of hostility on their part whatever, only of intense and expectant interest in me and what I might do. As I opened the door of the car the comic aspect of the situation struck me forcibly and I burst out laughing. I am afraid my little black friends were sadly lacking in a sense of humor, for my amusement had not the slightest effect on them. I drove off just as I had come, gradually edging them out of my way; they silently and, it almost seemed, reluctantly hopped aside to let me pass. I had not gone fifty yards beyond the last of the birds on the road when the full-throated roar of the cawing broke out again.

I want to be quite clear that I am not suggesting that anything was at all occult in all this. It may or may not have been so. I can say, however, that never before in my life had I seen so many rooks gathered together in one place; indeed, I would not hazard a guess how many rookeries were represented there. As most countrymen know, every now and again rooks do congregate together in amazing numbers, with great noise and seemingly aimless activity. Why they do so, no one seems to know; at least

I have never heard any satisfactory explanation. I may have come across some such gathering—a very big and important one—as a mere coincidence, but even so, the behavior of the birds remains to be explained, and I feel that, taking everything together, it was all very unusual. Let me leave it at that. None the less, my little black stone is a precious memento of that excursion.

The fairy lights on this particular field have been seen a number of times by other people. Only a few years ago a Mrs. McNicholas—Anna-Maria of our childhood days— who lived not far from the Shanachuee cross and in sight of the fairy ground, saw them clearly. As she watched, they left the field and she saw them travel in a line along the brow of a long, low hill till they disappeared among the trees of Rathlevin, about a mile away. This was about 9:00 or 10:00 o'clock in the evening.

THE CRILLAUN FAIRY LIGHTS

Indeed, the seeing of fairy lights as my mother saw them is more frequent than might be supposed. There is a small fairy fort not so very far from Castlebar which rises north of a little lough that is not more than three quarters of a mile wide. To the southeast of the lough is another even smaller fairy fort, while to the south of it and not one hundred yards from the shore is a farmhouse. The first fort is called Crillaun, and in the neighborhood it has always been known to be a busy center of fairy activity. From time to time the fort has been seen ablaze with little twinkling lights. They are said to move from one fort to another sometimes, though this is rare. Generation after generation has known of this and has passed on the knowledge to the next, and in each generation some people have seen these lights and have added their knowledge to the lore of the past.

I know three charming, well-educated, and very intelligent ladies who in their youth lived in this farmhouse near the lough, and a short while ago I sought them out for further information. In the course of my questions I asked one, Miss Diana, why she was so sure upon some point, whereupon she told me that she herself had seen them twice a few years ago, when she was in her early twenties, though there was a gap of three or four years between each "seeing." On each occasion the circumstances were much the same. She watched them from a window, for a long time on one occasion, but not so long the second time, as she then felt rather nervous.

The first time it was about mid-November, the next time earlier in the year, perhaps August. She saw the lights very distinctly on each occasion. Both nights were calm and clear, and the time was between 9:00 and 10:00 P.M. The lights were of many colors—red, green, blue, yellow—and they were as bright and steady as electric lights would be.

Then I found that her sister, Miss Patricia, had seen them once and, what was most interesting, she had seen them move. She was about eighteen at the time and was outside the house on November Eve, or, as we at home call it, Hallowe'en. It was round about 9:00 o'clock at night, and as she walked back to the house from whatever she had gone to do outside, her attention was at once caught by the bright illumination across the lough. She stared in amazement, for there was the little fort brightly lit up with hundreds of little white lights. It is interesting

to note that each time Miss Diana saw these lights they
were all of bright colors, while those that Miss Patricia
saw were, without exception, white.

But if Miss Patricia was astonished at first, it was
nothing to her utter amazement when she saw them all
rise up as one and, keeping their formation, sail steadily
through the air across the little lough towards the other
fort, not far from the farmhouse. She did not see them
settle there; indeed, she did not dream of waiting to see
them settle, but very naturally she hastily retreated to the
safety of the house.

WILL-O'-THE-WISP

These "seeings" are exceedingly interesting and fit
in exactly with the tradition of the place. The lights could
not possibly be Will-o'-the-Wisp or any form of ignis
fatuus, for several very potent reasons. In the first place,
ignis fatuus is white, while on two occasions these fairy
lights were seen clearly to be brightly colored. Then marsh
gas, or methane, can never stay still for long, for the slight
heat which it generates causes it to create air movements
which stir it from place to place, and so it must always
move. Finally, it is not possible for this gas to rise in the
air and pass over a wide stretch of water, and it is quite
fantastic to suggest that a large number of balls of gas
could do so simultaneously and keep their formation. No.
Some other explanation must be sought and it seems to me
that the traditional one is less outrageous to common sense
than farfetched "natural" ones.

Now that we are on the subject, Will-o'-the-Wisp or
jack-o'-lantern or whatever one chooses to call it is a very
interesting phenomenon of the country. In all my life I

have seen it only three times, twice clearly and closely and once more distantly and vaguely. It is presumably marsh gas, or methane, which is generated by the rotting vegetation of the bogs and swamps and which under certain conditions gives off light. I have seen it asserted in responsible books and works of reference that it ignites spontaneously, but it seems to me that this requires some qualification. It is never a burning flame, but a compact ball of light constantly on the move, and so it can have no source from which to renew itself as flame requires.

I know a countryman whose work takes him out after dark a good deal and who has on two occasions actually touched it, finding no appreciable heat and most certainly no burning. As we know, Will-o'-the-Wisp, usually the size of a large football, will go bouncing along over a marsh from tuft to tuft, giving the impression from a distance of someone carrying a bright light. Sometimes it will hit a tuft especially hard and break up into a number of little balls the size of tennis or golf balls. These in their turn go bouncing along but soon dissipate and disappear.

On one occasion my friend was walking along a very narrow track across a bog, one that he knew so well that he was in no danger of losing it in the starry night, though he had no light himself. Suddenly he saw a Will-o'-the-Wisp hopping along towards him. It soon came so close that he kicked out at it and broke it up into a number of smaller balls which went dancing on till they disappeared after twenty yards or so. But some globules or patches of light remained on his trousers, and in fear of getting singed, he brushed them off with his hand. But the light went out as he brushed, and he felt little or no heat on his hand.

Another time, he was going home about 10:00 P.M.

along the newly metaled road from Pontoon to Laherdaun
when he saw what he took to be a single headlight of a
parked car on the road, but as he got nearer he saw that
the whole road was covered to a depth of about eighteen
inches with a bright misty light. It covered only the
metaled road and did not extend to the grass or ditches
on either side. It was quite stationary, and he stood looking at it for some time, wondering what on earth to do.
An almost universal maxim in the West of Ireland, when
anything does not work, says to "hit it a kick," and accordingly this is what he did. As he withdrew his leg he
saw that a number of "lumps" of light still adhered to his
trousers, but they brushed off easily. He tried again, and
with the same satisfactory result; then he took his courage
in both hands and walked quickly through the light, easily
sweeping all trace of it off as soon as he emerged on the
other side, and happily made his way home.

This is a very curious incident, and I have no doubt
about his general accuracy. However, it shows the gas
behaving quite differently to the normal. There must have
been something in the newly tarred surface of the road to
hold the gas in a way that never happens and cannot
happen in a bog or marsh where Will-o'-the-Wisp properly belongs.

There are all sorts of curious lights to be seen in the
country. When walking across a boggy place one can
sometimes see clear phosphorescence wherever the hob-
nails or iron toe and heel tips of one's boots have been.
Some timbers, especially birch, can give off a strong glow
at night. I know a man who went to get some logs from
his woodshed one night, and when he opened the door
the glowing silvery light from the logs was enough to
enable him to make out every detail in the shed.

Many countrymen, of course, put Will-o'-the-Wisp down to fairy agency entirely, and even when one assures them that it is marsh gas, they point out that it does things that are almost of human thought.

A very intelligent and well-balanced girl I know told me how, one night as she was walking home only an hour or so after dark, she saw a Will-o'-the-Wisp moving slowly along the bog parallel with the road and not fifty yards away. She stopped to have a good look at it, assuring herself that it was only gas and that there were no such things as fairies. But as soon as she stopped to look at it, it suddenly changed course and began to come straight towards her, increasing its speed. This rather shook her determination to examine it with scientific coolness, so she hastily moved down the road a bit. To her consternation it changed direction too and still came straight for her, now crossing the soft bog as fast as a man could run on a road. This proved to be too great a strain on her morale and she, very excusably, I think, promptly turned and made for home with all the speed she could. To this day, she is convinced that it was directed by a real intelligence.

But if spirits of nature do exist, it seems reasonable that they should sometimes utilize and direct as they wish such a truly natural phenomenon as our familiar Will-o'-the-Wisp, just as we can direct a car. It is an interesting speculation.

THE RATHMORE FORT

In the townland of Rathmore, between Tralee and Killarney, there is a curious fort with three concentric circles instead of the usual single bank and ditch. It is by the side of the River Maine and it is not a complete circle, for the banks run only about two thirds of the way round the arc of the circle, the bank of the river forming a secant cutting off the rest. Clearly there once were three complete rings, but the small outer one has largely vanished in the course of time, so that it is now difficult to trace it all the way. The next bank is quite substantial, steep-sided and high, while the inner one is some ten feet wide, flattish on top and only a couple of feet high. There are about twelve feet of level ground between the two inner banks.

Some fifty years ago, on a sunny day in July, the owner of the land, a farmer, O'Sullivan by name, had been mowing the four acres or so which were enclosed by this fort for meadowing. He was annoyed, as he had been each previous year, because he could not get his two horses and the mowing machine to work in the narrow space between the two banks. This was all the more disappointing as it held fine lush grass and it would again be a tedious job cutting it all by hand with a scythe; measured all the way round, there was a lot of ground to be covered. As he looked at the small inner bank, he thought to himself how easy it would be if only it were not there. Then he thought of his two fine, lusty sons, eighteen and twenty-two years of age. They could level it in no time, and make light work of it too. There was a big hole in the next field, possibly the source of the earth forming one of the fort rings, and this could be filled with advantage.

That decided him, so the next morning he sent his two sons up with a horse and cart to get ahead with the work without delay. They duly set to with a will, and after filling two or three cartloads and dumping them in the hollow, they sat down on the bank to rest a few minutes while they lit their pipes. It is important to remember that they had the horse and cart close by them.

Although it was warm and sunny, quite a breeze was blowing across the open hill, and so, to light their pipes, they turned their backs to the wind and bent down over their cupped hands, while they busily puffed and drew the pipes safely alight. It took them no more than thirty seconds. Then they righted themselves and sat staring before them with horrified astonishment, and small wonder. There was the cart beside them, certainly, but with no horse in it and its shafts resting securely on the ground, while at a short distance away they saw the horse itself quietly grazing as if nothing had happened. Everyone knows how noisy a horse and cart must be in every movement it makes, with the jingling of chains, the flapping of harness, the creaking of axle, and the stamping and snorting of horse. But all this had been done without the slightest sound to warn the brothers of the weird spectacle now confronting them.

Here was unexpected intervention by the unseen world which could not be ignored, and neither of the lads was in the slightest doubt as to its meaning. It was an unmistakable but fortunately a very gentle and kindly warning not to tamper further with or desecrate in any way this fort now clearly appropriated to the fairies' use. It is not surprising, then, that in a few moments the boys were on their way home with the horse and cart. When they told their adventures to their father, their quite obvious sincerity and distress soon convinced him of the truth of their story. That bank still remains inviolate to this very day and can be seen at any time by the sufficiently curious.

The Stray Sod

Give me your hand! So, keeping close to me,
Shut tight your eyes! Step forward!
—Where are we?

James Stephens

Foidin Seachrain, the "stray sod" or, as it is called in some localities, the "lone sod," is a very well-known and long-established proceeding in Ireland. Many other countries throughout the world have similar traps for the unwary—or for anyone who puts himself within its range. In Ireland it is merely harmless and annoying, but I have come across some African and Indian variations that can be hurtful and vicious in no small degree. The most generally held view of it round my home is that the fairies sometimes put a spell on a piece of earth, usually a sod of grass, and whoever inadvertently steps upon it loses his way at once and cannot find an exit from

144

whatever place he is in, whether field or wood or open bog, until the fairies tire of their game and at last throw open the unseen doors.

It is also widely believed that one can counter the spell by turning one's coat inside out and so wearing it, but I have never heard of any authentic case where this has been done successfully. When two or more people are together and the leader seems uncertain of the way, and you fear that he has stepped on the fatal stray sod you say to him in Irish, "Will thu ceart?" ("Are you right?"). If he answers, "Nil iosagam" ("I don't know") and then adds "Taim a' gol amu" ("I think I am going astray"), you quickly reply, "The Lord save you" and then make the sign of the cross. It is maintained that to work effectively all this must be spoken in Irish. However, I know of two cases where this was tried as well as turning the coat, but all quite unsuccessfully.

Here are two fully authenticated occurrences, in both of which, though held prisoner for hours, the victims were not lost, inasmuch as it was always perfectly clear where they were all the time, but they just could not get out.

THE GATELESS FIELD

The Reverend Mr. Harris was rector of a parish which was officially in County Leitrim but which in fact overflowed into both Sligo and Roscommon, for the rectory was near where the three counties meet. Indeed, the blacksmith's forge was reputed to be exactly in that spot, so that it was partly in each of the three counties. Mr. Harris had been there a number of years when this incident took place, and he was liked and respected everywhere. It is as well to make it clear that, though full of human sympathy and understanding, Mr. Harris was a very practical, matter-of-fact, and energetic man, the very antithesis of a dreamy, airy-fairy romantic.

On Midsummer's Day in 1916 he received a call to visit a sick parishioner who lived about seven miles away by road from the rectory. There was a footpath over the hills which would save him nearly four miles, or over half the distance that it was by road. It was an attractive path and one which he knew well, for he had used it often. As it was a beautiful clear evening, he decided to walk over the fields along this pleasant footpath and so avoid the bother of taking out the horse and trap. It was just after 10:00 o'clock when he started and, telling his wife he would be back shortly after midnight, he set off confidently at a swinging pace, striding along the route he knew so well.

At one place, about three quarters of a mile from the rectory, the bridle path crosses a seven-acre field, in the middle of which stands a large thorn tree, ancient and weatherbeaten and locally reputed to be adopted by the fairy folk. The path leads into this field by a strong five-barred wooden gate, full-sized and well capable of admitting a farm horse and cart. At the other side it leaves the field by a stile. The field is surrounded by a bank surmounted by a thick and impenetrable thorn hedge, inside which there is a deep ditch.

Mr. Harris arrived at the gate and passed through it, carefully closing it after him as a good countryman should, and then went on unconcernedly towards the stile. But to his astonishment when he got there, there was no stile, and then he noticed that there was no path either. Thinking he must have wandered off the path while musing deeply, he walked down the hedge to reach the stile. It was quite reasonably light, and he looked up and down the hedge and saw there was no stile anywhere, and no path at all. By this time he began to realize that something supernatural was at work, but his only feelings were a mixture of amusement and annoyance and not the slightest fear. Nor did he sense anything evil or hostile, but only chuckling, impish mischievousness somewhere in the background.

So he gave up trying to find the stile and went back to the gate, deciding to try another route, but when he got to the gate he received a greater shock still for there *was* no gate nor any path to it either! He looked round him in bewilderment. There was the field all about him, its thick thorn hedge black and solid in the dim light. There was the hoary old fairy tree looming up in the center, but nowhere was there any gate or stile or path. The thing seemed utterly and fantastically absurd, but there it was and it could not be ignored. However, he refused to accept defeat, so he set to work and systematically walked along every hedge, scanning every foot closely but futilely for any opening at all. In due course he arrived back at the point from which he had started and became completely nonplussed. Now there could be no doubt about it, there was no way out!

It is difficult to say how long this impasse continued, but probably it was for a couple of hours, during which time Mr. Harris unceasingly kept up his search for an exit. Suddenly the spell was lifted, the unseen bars were raised, and Mr. Harris found both gate and stile again where they should have been all the time. Indeed, he found himself standing quite close to the stile. The joke was over, the fairies had had their fun, and now he was free to continue on his way. All the same, Mr. Harris did not for a moment forget that he had a duty to do toward a sick parishioner and, for all he knew, some other fairies might play a similar trick on him as he walked over the wilder hills that still lay before him. To be on the safe side, feeling that discretion was the wiser course, he returned to the rectory. As it was by then too late to turn out the trap, he got out his bicycle and went on his way by road. Seven miles by road, he decided, was perhaps shorter than any distance through fairy fields.

This field, with its gate and stile and fairy thorn, can be seen today if anyone should like to risk a walk through it on Midsummer Eve or Night or Beltane, or any other fairy time.

THE LIS ARD SPELL

In 1935, my aunt, then the occupant for life of our family home in Mayo, required a companion-help for her nurse-housekeeper. With some care she chose a very nice, intelligent, and steady girl of nineteen, B.M., who came from a respected family of prosperous small farmers in the little townland of Meelich, about three or four miles away to the north. This girl had never left home before and so, under my aunt's meticulous care, her life continued to be sheltered and controlled. She was introduced to three or four of the leading local farmers, all ex-tenants and family friends and supporters of ours of many generations, and her visits were restricted to them. Particularly included in this select list was the very respected family of the nurse-housekeeper's, under whose immediate charge the girl was.

One Saturday, after her first six or seven weeks at the Big House, having the afternoon off, she decided to spend it with the Solons, the housekeeper's family. As it was a bright, sunny day and she was feeling rather homesick, she thought she would first climb Lis Ard, the famous fairy fort, which was less than a quarter of a mile behind the house and not much out of her road to the Solons'. From it, she could look across the country and see the roofless Round Tower of Meelich. She was to be back in the house by 7:00 P.M., in time for the evening meal and long before darkness would set in. But at 7:00 o'clock she had not returned, and when at 8:00 o'clock there was still no sign of her, a messenger was dispatched to the farm. He soon returned with the alarming news that she had never been there, and it did not take much longer to get the same replies from all the other cottages in the neighborhood.

Then, indeed, the alarm became serious, and as by this time it was dark, several search parties provided with lanterns were at once organized to scour the surrounding country thoroughly. The search was prosecuted vigorously for several hours, and not till between 11:00 P.M. and midnight did the various parties come back to the Big House, having by then abandoned their efforts as hopeless.

Only a few minutes after the last party returned, B.M. herself walked through the open hall door and sank on to a settee, where she burst into tears. It was clear the poor girl was in a state of utter exhaustion and nervous strain, but she was young and healthy and the warmth of the kitchen fire and a good hot cup of strong tea soon made her all right again.

The story she had to tell was astonishing, and the neighbors listened spellbound as she unfolded her adventures, the lilt of her soft country voice dominating the room. It seems that on her way to the Solons' she had

walked off as she had planned to the left across the fields
to the foot of Lis Ard. All went well as she climbed its
steep slopes, clambered over the surrounding bank,
crossed the ditch, and made her way through the beech
wood covering its center till she reached the summit. It
was a lovely summer's day and she stood and looked between the trees out and across the country to admire distant Nephin raising its majestic and solid bulk away to
the northwest. Then her eyes wandered nearer home till
she saw due north the roofless Round Tower of Meelich,
till recently the center of her youthful life. Though she
could not make out for certain her own home, yet all the
distant features—woods, bogs, and hillocks—were plucking at her heart strings. For some time she gazed at them,
then she looked down beneath her at the small farms and
cottages nestling snugly by their lanes, one of which was
now her destination. She followed with her eyes the winding back avenue as it passed field and wood till it merged
into the road which led to these small, tidy farms.

She felt a little chilly now. Though it was nearly summer, her thin new frock, a nice red shot-silk one sent to
her by relatives in America, was no protection from the
cool hill breezes. So she walked down gaily towards a gap
in the outer bank—and as she reached it the incredible
took place. She had just got to the opening when she felt
a queer kind of jerk, a muscular jerk inside her rather than
from outside, and before she realized what had happened
she found herself walking quickly towards the center of
the wood again, and in exactly the opposite direction.

It was a moment or two before she could collect her
wits sufficiently to stop herself and turn again. As yet, she
had not the slightest idea of anything supernormal, but
just smiled to herself at her silly mistake, as she imagined

it to be, and started off again for the same gap. But when she reached it, exactly the same thing happened and in exactly the same way. Then indeed astonishment seized her, soon to give way to fear.

She stood a few moments, looking about her and fighting back the panic rising in her breast. As she looked at the quiet, friendly wood around her and the smiling sunny countryside beyond and beneath it, her panic left her and she tossed her head and boldly stepped out again, this time making for the point on the bank where she had entered. She tried to climb over it here, and it looked quite easy, for the ditch was shallow and the bank was low. But now she received her greatest shock, for she felt as if an invisible wall was there which she could not pass. Whether it was all just in her mind or whether it was an invisible objective structure, she cannot to this day be sure, but it was none the less a fact that along that bank there was a line which she was quite unable to pass, unable even to stretch her arm across.

She walked along the ditch to her right, her breath catching in deep gasps that were very near to sobs as she tried again and again to cross that eerie line, fortifying herself with an intensity of prayer, but all to no purpose. After stumbling along the ditch over stones and roots for some distance, she stopped and turned back to the top of the rise. She felt strongly within herself that it would be fatal for her to sit or lie down or to relax in any way before this unseen power, but that she must keep herself alert and active, ready to take the first chance of escape without a moment's delay, or worse might well befall her.

And now the feeling of serene friendliness which she had felt before from the surrounding fort left her, and she

sensed with ever-growing intensity a feeling of hostility
and personal resentment flooding towards her like an angry mountain stream in spate. It came, she was sure, from
some point on the northwest edge of the fort, but beyond
that conviction she was quite mystified. However, she
kept as far away from it as she could, down by the bank
and gaps to the southeast, round the point where she had
entered.

At last the sun began to set and twilight came on, to
be followed only too rapidly by the darkness of a moon-
less night, the utter, impenetrable blackness of which
country people know so well. Like a wild animal in a
cage, she kept moving up and down that stretch of ditch
and probing the bank in a ceaseless effort to find a way
through the magic wall which inexorably shut her in. Soon
coldness and tiredness added their weight to her distress,
and at last she saw a lantern bobbing up and down in the
distance. It came steadily nearer, and in a short time she
could make out the figures of three or four men. As they
came nearer still, she shouted and called at the top of her
voice in a frenzy of hopeful excitement. They came nearer
and nearer and she could hear their voices calling—in answer, she hopefully thought, to her own cries. They came
up the hill and walked along outside the bank, waving the
lantern and calling her name, indeed at one time they
were not more than twenty or thirty yards from her. By
this time she was standing on the high ground just inside
the ditch, in full view, while she desperately called to
them, but they passed on, unable to see or hear her
through that magic wall standing invisibly between them.
So they moved away, leaving her behind and still power-
less in her invisible prison.

It was too dark for her to move except with great care,

and as soon as this party had left, she could only return to her restless groping up and down the dry ditch, always looking for a way out. In this darkness time seemed interminable, the silent monotony being broken twice by the more distant sight of two other search parties moving along with their swinging lights.

At last another party appeared, moving past the bottom of the hill on its way back to the house. It was too far away for a hail, and she was looking at it wistfully when she suddenly realized that the invisible barrier to her had disappeared. At once, without any further trouble she clambered out through a gap and stood for a moment on the dark slope of the hill exulting with thankfulness to heaven that now she was really free. But she did not yet feel safe, so she lost no time in following the lantern before her. Having to move gingerly in the dark, she could not overtake the party. No one heard her calls, so she gave up hailing and concentrated all her energies on getting down safely to the path that ran at the foot of the hill. Once on it, she lost no time, as can well be imagined, in making her way back to the house.

No reasonable person listening to her could doubt her story, and though she was closely questioned, she never deviated once even in a detail, nor has she ever done so since. No house had received her that day, for such a possibility was checked up again and again. There could be no doubt at all about her physical exhaustion, which was inevitable after standing such long hours and in such distress. That her cotton frock was quite clean, unstained, and uncreased was further evidence that she had not slept or rested anywhere. Today she is the godly and respected mother of a family and is as convincing as ever concerning the truth and accuracy of her story.

MIKE'S ADVENTURE

When I was a boy there was an amusing case of
the stray sod in a field that separated two houses on the
Killeaden estate. One house belonged to John Solon and
the other was the little cottage of beloved Nancy Cun-
ningham, my father's nurse and a prodigious spoiler of me
in later years. Her nephew, Mike Walshe, would sometimes stay with her.

Mike, who could take a drop on occasion, though very
far indeed from being a drunkard, was for various reasons
rather a joke round about, but was popular none the less,
for he was friendly and never harmed anyone.

One evening at John's house there was a happy social
party but no drink at all. The party broke up early, about
10:00 P.M., and Mike, who was there, set out across the
intervening field to return to Nancy's cottage. Midnight
was well past when John's family was awakened by violent hammerings on the door. When the door was at last
flung open, poor Mike staggered in, a woebegone figure
indeed, with his old coat on him inside out and soaked to
the skin with wet. He was shivering with cold and exhaustion and could hardly speak. The fire was soon fanned
to a blaze and a hot drink made for him, and he crouched
on a stool warming himself gratefully over the glowing
coals of turf.

Only then did he begin to reply to all the urgent questions put to him. He told how he had set off across the single field before him and how he had not gone far till he
realized he was in a strange place and not in the field he
knew at all. So he immediately took off his coat, turned it

inside out and put it on like that, but unfortunately this did not help him in the least, for wherever he went, whichever way he turned, he found himself faced by an unknown and impenetrable fence.

Eventually, in despair he crouched down against a bank to wait, but for how long he could not tell, though it seemed ages till, rendered desperate by cold and stiffness, he decided to have another effort to get out. This time all went well, and finding himself near the house he had left, he went back to it for help and shelter. He was not drunk in the least for, poor fellow, he had had nothing to drink. What other kind of mental state he had got into is anybody's guess, but when found by the Solons he was quite coherent, though in a condition of mental and physical distress, which seems quite reasonable under the circumstances.

But far from getting sympathy for his woes, poor man, he got well laughed at, and Mike and the fairies became a byword for a long time.

POACHERS ASTRAY

A favorite sport among the lads of the countryside in the old days was poaching salmon at night on the river. A sod of turf would be well soaked in paraffin and then securely impaled on a pitchfork or anything like it that was handy. Then, at likely places in the river, the turf was lit and the blazing torch was held over the water, the lads wading to and fro in the shallows till a fish was seen. It would be dazzled and stupefied by the bright light and so would be easily speared and thrown ashore. But none of this could be done in secret, for the blazing light pro-

claimed far and wide that poachers were abroad, and so
the "bargers," as the water bailiffs were called, would get
out after them.

This was the real fun of it, and without this added excitement it would have been looked upon as poor sport.
Chased closely enough by the bargers, the lads would
eventually extinguish the torch by plunging it into the
river and disperse across the fields in the dark, regather-
ing for a meal and a discussion of their adventures in some
previously appointed local cottage. If any salmon had
been taken, they would be brought along and divided.

On one occasion a piper who had been invited by a
local relative to come in from some miles away and who
knew the ground well, never turned up at the rendezvous.
He must have stepped on the stray sod, for it was not till
hours later that a search party found him crouched against
a bank, utterly lost and without any idea of his whereabouts. As soon as he was found he got his proper bearings again at once, so it must have been their arrival that
broke the spell that was holding him.

Lismirrane

Just beyond the Killeaden boundary and on the
same side of the river there is a fort called Lismirrane,
under which nestle a schoolhouse and several neighboring
houses. The name means "the fort of the place where people are put astray," and it can be seen that the tradition
of the stray sod is firmly rooted all round that country.

Of course, one does not have to be unduly cynical to
see that the stray sod can be a God-sent excuse to a belated home comer who has been celebrating out not wisely

but too well. But the experience rarely if ever happens to tipplers and is inflicted rather upon decent, sensible, sober people. From the fairies' point of view there would, surely, be little fun in it otherwise.

CHAPTER IX

Hostile Spirits and Hurtful Spells

Crossing the shallow holding and high above the sea
Where few birds nest, the luckless foot may pass
From the bright safety of experience
Into the terror of the hungry grass.

Donagh McDonagh

THE FAIRY HUNGER

The "fear gortach," or "hungry grass," is decidedly unpleasant. It is fairly common in certain districts though rare in others. I suppose the degree of its prevalence depends upon the predilections of the local fairies, though I have heard people say that it is nothing to do with the fairies at all but occurs only where an uncoffined corpse has been laid on its way to a burial. Others, and they are the majority, deny this vigorously as

almost impious and are firm in associating it entirely with
the fairies.

It is hurtful, all right, but I never heard of it harming
anyone. Its effect is very temporary and is easily cured by
enough food. It is sometimes quite local, and there was a
part of the road passing the old Ormsby estate of Ballina-
more, a few miles west of Kiltimagh, where people at one
time were so frequently struck with it on their way to
town that a bowl of stirabout was kept handy by the
woman of a house nearby, and many are the sufferers she
helped by that kindly thoughtfulness. The worst day of
the whole year for the hungry grass to strike a person here
was May Day.

One thoroughly verified account of it occurred near
my home. During the years that Lord Aberdeen was Lord-
Lieutenant of Ireland and lived in Vice-Regal Lodge in
the Phoenix Park, my aunt, Miss Emma Mac Manus, became a close friend of Lady Aberdeen's and a collaborator
with her in many of her works for the benefit of the
country. Arising out of this, Miss Emma decided to hold
an agricultural show in the grounds of our home, Killeaden House. This caused a good deal of interest, as it
was the first of its kind to be held in County Mayo, and
Miss Emma hoped it might encourage others to do like-
wise. It took place in 1915, and in the early summer of
that year she selected a committee of local shopkeepers
and small farmers to assist her in organizing it.

Mr. Michael Murphy, the largest shopkeeper and most
respected citizen of the local town of Kiltimagh, was appointed Honorary Treasurer. He took up his duties with
energy, being then forty-eight and in his vigorous prime.
It was lovely warm weather, and my aunt often held her

committee meetings in the well-built two-roomed stone
garden house. This stood on a rise in the five-acre orchard
and was overshadowed by great forest beeches, the home
of many wood pigeons, red squirrels, tree creepers, and all
sorts of fascinating woodland life.

On the particular occasion of this story she called a
meeting of the show committee for 8:00 P.M. in the garden
house. Present were not only my aunt and a lady friend
then staying with her, but also the poultry and horti-
cultural instructresses for the county; Mr. Murphy, the
Treasurer; Mr. McNicholas, the Honorary Secretary, who
was also a local schoolmaster, and two or three other
locals of the same kind. Mr. Murphy, after having consumed a full and well-supplied high tea at his home, left at
7:45 in the evening and leisurely cycled the three miles to
Killeaden. The meeting took its usual quiet course and
ended at 10:00 P.M., when my aunt supplied them all
with a good tea, which included plenty of sandwiches and
buns.

Mr. Murphy and Mr. McNicholas left together, and at
the avenue gates they parted, going in opposite directions.
But Mr. Murphy had not cycled thirty yards when he
was suddenly attacked with a violent hunger. The hunger
seemed to move into him like an active physical thing
from the bog on his right, and with every yard he pedaled
it became worse and worse, gnawing and twisting his inside with excruciating pangs. By the time he reached the
river bridge he had become so weak and so racked with
these pangs of hunger that he could cycle no more. He
stopped and half dismounted, half fell from his cycle,
staggering to the wall of the bridge to rest awhile before
starting his never-to-be-forgotten struggle to get home.
From the bridge it is a gentle uphill incline all the two and

a half miles to the town and, pushing and leaning on his cycle for support, he fought his way along till at last he reached the main street of the town. Coming to his own door, he dropped his cycle and staggered in, calling urgently for food. He entered his dining room and promptly collapsed on his face upon the hearth rug. His alarmed family hastily attended to him, handing him a large quartern loaf fresh and hot from the oven and a dish of butter. He could not wait to cut it, but before their astonished faces he tore it into pieces and devoured it plain and unbuttered, nor did he cease till the whole loaf was consumed to the last crumb.

Only then did his strength begin to return and, though still rather weak and shaky, he got up and took his proper place at the table. Still avidly hungry, he next set to work and ate another full meal of ham and eggs and potatoes and milk. He eventually satisfied this mysterious and over-whelming hunger and told his family of his adventures. He then began to think of the consequences. His digestion was not too strong, and the result of ravenously devouring a whole large loaf of hot bread seemed certain to be alarming, and a restless night of indigestion and gripes surely lay before him. However, he began to feel extremely drowsy and soon went to bed. Far from having a bad night, he fell asleep at once, slept soundly and restfully all night, and awoke the next morning feeling as fresh and well as could be.

This fairy hunger is a curious thing and is well known in Ireland, though I have never heard of it in other countries. It comes on suddenly when one is in some lonely country place, and it is too fierce to be resisted. It is temporary and has no lasting ill effects. In this case, Mr. Murphy must have absorbed an enormous amount of food, what with his normal high tea, my aunt's generous refreshments, and all that he ate when he staggered home.

Here are four stories of demons. The first two, I give in spite of the fact that the people concerned are now dead, because they are well authenticated and are personal to me, and I have known of them so well all my life. Indeed, it would be hard to find any story better authenticated than are these four.

THE ORCHARD ELEMENTAL

This occurrence took place in the late sixties of the last century when my uncles and aunts were in their teens or in young manhood and womanhood. One summer night they gave a party in the garden house which I have previously described and which stood at the farther end of the orchard. Here they could be as gay and make as much noise as they liked without disturbing the house, all the more important as a friend of my grandmother's was feeling poorly and in bed at the time.

It was during the height of summer and the youngsters, having invited friends of their own age from various houses in the county, worked hard all day bringing up supplies and getting everything ready. My grandmother had laid it down that they must make all the preparations themselves and not take any of the men or maids off their ordinary work. In due course all was ready and after supper they trooped up and started their party, which was a huge success.

Shortly before midnight, when it was getting on for their time to return, my grandfather thought he would stroll up and see how they had prospered, first playing a joke on them by hammering on the door and windows and pretending he was a ghost or some other uncanny thing. The moon was nearly full and was high in the sky, though there was some wind, and light clouds were scudding across the sky, making the night a little less bright than it might have been.

My grandfather took his stick and walked out by the old garden, across the back avenue, and through the haggard into the dark bottom of the orchard behind the stables. The darkness was profound as he went under some large holm oaks and along a line of huge beeches till at last he emerged halfway up to the garden house. On his left, there was a dense clump of laurels and on his right a small open space after which came the apple trees, all large and old, making it dark enough under their thick leaves.

As he reached the glade, he heard the rustle of dry leaves among the laurels and a large animal ran out, crossing from his left to his right towards the apple trees. It was not three paces from him and he saw it clearly. It was the shape of a fox with a large bushy tail, but of enormous size, more like a wolf than a fox. As it reached the glade he clapped his hands and called, "Shoo!", whereat it stopped at once, stood up on its hind legs, and turned to face him. It was his own height or more, but to his horror he saw it had no head. In spite of that, he knew it was looking at him and pouring out hate, bestiality, and evil.

For what seemed an age he stood spellbound, facing it and looking at where its eyes should have been, but he saw nothing. He could see clearly, and realized he was seeing, the apple tree behind it, where its head should have been, where its head *was* but could not be seen, though he felt the baleful hate that poured out from it.

At last he pulled himself together and, raising his hand, made the sign of the cross, calling all the powers of heaven to his aid. At this, it dropped on its four legs again and, turning, ran away swiftly into the darkness of the apple trees, where it disappeared. That was enough for my grandfather and, brave as he was, he decided that it was no night for playing ghostly tricks with such things abroad, so he turned and went home again, going the longer but less dark way by the front avenue. He thought it unnecessary to upset the happy party, for ten or twelve gay young men and women coming back with lights and laughter would be more than a match for any elemental.

When he returned to the house, he told my grandmother about his adventure, but not till some months later did he mention it to any of his children. Many years later, after his death, I heard the details from my father and my aunts. In 1901, when my grandfather lay dying in his house in Worthing on the south coast of England, my Aunt Lottie, who was deeply interested in these matters, reminded him of this incident. Though ninety-one years old, he remembered it clearly. So she got pen and paper and took down his full account of it in his own words and then handed it to him for his signature. He knew well that he was dying, and it was the last time he signed his name, for he died the next day. I have seen that statement myself and it is today among my aunt's papers.

THE STABLE DEMON

My father told me not once but several times of an eerie and unpleasant experience he had when he was a boy of about fourteen and was home for the Christmas holidays from his English school. He was playing hide and seek with his elder brother, Arthur, but the game was confined to the large square of the stable buildings, including the cow byres, granaries, haylofts, and all the rest. It was late afternoon and not yet dark outside, when my father, tiptoeing stealthily along a granary, heard a noise of trampling, plunging, and snorting from one of the stables below. In those days there were two trap doors above the manger of each stable, one at each end, from which the men could throw down hay more easily.

Going quickly to one of the trap doors above the noisy stable, my father pulled it open suddenly, hoping to catch his brother, and thrust his head down through it before jumping down himself. But to his astonishment he saw the two horses in a mad panic of terror, trembling and snorting with fear as they tried to get as far away as they could from something in the manger at the far end from my father and, perhaps fortunately for him, right under the other trap door. Amazed, he looked across and saw, not twelve feet from his head, something that filled him with horror—a sight that he never forgot all the days of his life. For there he saw a crouching figure of evil with blazing red, baleful eyes like glowing coals of fire. It was huddled in a compact ball, as a boy of his own size might look when squatting on his haunches. My father remembered only those awful eyes, the squatness of the body hunched in the dark corner of the manger, and one awful hand, a human hand, but how different! It gripped the edge of the manger and was a dirty grayish-brown. The fingers were all bone and sinew and ended not in human nails but in curved and pointed claws.

The boy's breath nearly stopped, and after staring at it in ghastly fascination, he hurled himself back into the granary again, slammed down the trap door, and raced for the house, calling to warn his brother first. Luckily, almost at his first shout his brother came and they both hurried back to the bedroom they shared, where my father told what he had seen.

Many years later, when I was nearly seven and long before I had heard this story, I was returning with my father one summer evening from the orchard, where he had been helping me to fill my pockets with good eating apples, for he knew all the best trees well. Twilight was just beginning and, having passed under the shadows of the big holm oaks, we reached the haggard; indeed, we were halfway across it, and I was firmly clasping my father's hand, when he suddenly stopped and turned and made the sign of the cross in the air with the spud which he always carried for cutting thistles.

He made the sign three times towards the dark shadows of the orchard, and as we walked on, I said, "Daddy, why did you do that?" He hesitated a moment and then, clearly and impressively, replied, "There are things there that it is better to keep at a distance." I have never forgotten that little incident and most of all, perhaps, I have retained the realization of the strength and power of his fatherly love and of all the good that he stood for, vastly greater than any of those things that might try and harm me. I knew I was safe through him, utterly safe, and I never felt afraid there again.

THE CEMETERY POLTERGEIST

Some years ago there was a curious occurrence in a cemetery on the outskirts of Dublin, and although nothing very dramatic took place, it is so clearly occult and so well authenticated that it is well worth recording. The incident took place in the winter of 1935. The keeper of the cemetery was a Mrs. Dean, a woman of about fifty-five, whose husband was a confirmed invalid. At this time her mother was also in bed, seriously ill, indeed dying. Mrs. Dean herself was rather an eccentric woman, a "character," one might call her, for she was outspoken and frank, always ready with her tongue, perhaps too ready. One cold, clear, frosty night in January, with a full moon which shone on the white ground and threw back light till it was as bright as day, Dr. Sellars called to see Mrs. Dean's mother. He brought a young district nurse, Miss Sharp, to help him.

While the nurse was getting the patient ready in her bedroom, the doctor chatted with Mrs. Dean, for he had known them all for a number of years. But when he conventionally asked Mrs. Dean how she herself was getting on, he got the startling reply that she was having a lot of trouble recently. Then she casually jerked her thumb towards the cemetery and added, "It's the crowd out there. I wouldn't mind their being a bit fractious at first, but some will never settle down. And it's a good thing that X.Y. (mentioning a very prominent, influential, and wealthy citizen who had died some ten years before) is in a strong vault or he'd be worse than any of them with their antics."

Though the doctor had often heard her say some

curious things, this was beyond anything, and he was highly amused. Just then the young nurse returned to report that all was ready with the patient, but before going in, the doctor told her what Mrs. Dean had just said. The nurse, not knowing the caretaker so well, was rather impressed, but nursing came first and she went in to do her duty by her patient. In a few minutes she and the doctor were out again and about to leave. As the doctor struggled into his overcoat he mildly chaffed Mrs. Dean about her story, but she stood her ground and talked back at him. Saying good night to her, he went towards the door to the outside. Just as he reached the door, there was a terrific crash upon it, shaking it fiercely on its catch, and so violent was the blow that it might well have split the door from top to bottom. The doctor instantly put out his hand and threw it wide open, but outside all was quiet, serene, and bright under the full moon. He had been much too quick to allow anyone who might have knocked on the door to have had time to get away and disappear.

After he had carefully looked about to make sure there could be no one hiding, Dr. Sellars examined the door, expecting to find it badly damaged, but to his amazement there was not the slightest mark on it, not even a scratch. He turned back into the house to be met by a startled young nurse and a triumphant Mrs. Dean. "Didn't I tell you, now, doctor. Sure, that's what they do be annoying me with all the time." The doctor felt that things had got into too deep waters for comment without reflection, so he took the nurse home without more ado. However, he made a point of giving the door a very thorough examination the next morning, when he was able to go over it by daylight and at leisure, but that merely confirmed the fact that there was not the smallest scratch upon it.

I do not know why Mrs. Dean put the blame for her troubles on the dead in the cemetery, nor have I been able to get an explanation for her attitude from anyone who knew her. She has been dead herself some fifteen years now and has taken her knowledge with her. However, I feel quite certain she was mistaken, and that all these goings-on were coming from ill-natured earth spirits. Indeed, this crash on the door is a performance typical of poltergeists, though I have not yet been able to find out what exactly a poltergeist is meant to be. The word is entirely artificial and was coined in Germany about a century ago to cover this sort of manifestation. Dr. Sellars and the nurse are well and active at their professions today, and they remember this curious incident clearly.

The THING in the Doctor's Garden

Bleak Spike Island sits squarely in the middle of Cork Harbor, and as it faces the narrow entrance from the sea, it has always been of great importance to the defense of that famous naval port. Therefore, it is furnished with powerful batteries, strongly built stone barracks, and all the auxiliary buildings and dwellings necessary for accommodating those who are stationed there. For most of the year this bare little spot is windswept and cold, and one might think it unlikely it would ever have been inhabited but for its military importance. But it is, and its dwellers have little in the way of distraction. Before the

advent of wireless they must have been thrown back upon
their own thoughts a great deal too much, and the brood-
ing bareness of the place must have tended to make those
thoughts too often gloomy.

To those who claim to sense such things, the island
seems more suitably the abode of restless spirits and
savage demons than of normal and kindly human beings.
Long ago, tragedies took place there on dark and windy
nights: murders and suicides brought on by desperate
loneliness or drink, or, some say, by the urging of those
evil spirits who hate the presence of men invading their
isolated home.

That the demons still remain, in spite of human
habitation during the past two centuries and more, is
clearly shown by this story, which is related by Mrs.
Eileen Ganly, an artistic and charming lady well known
in the social life of Dublin. I have known her for many
years, and she is entirely sincere and reliable. Her narra-
tive can be taken at its face value as truly accurate and not
exaggerated in any way. I have heard her tell this story
over a number of years, and it has never varied, even
in detail.

The creature seen was clearly an elemental of a low
and very horrible kind, full of hostility towards humans,
and it might well have had a disastrous, even fatal, effect
on a sensitive little girl if she had seen it in all its dark
foulness. Her heart might have stopped if their eyes had
actually met.

The scene can be imagined easily. The small girl
skipping along merrily, her thoughts busy with happy
and simple childish things as she goes on her errand in
the bright, warm sunshine, when a stark horror suddenly
looms before her. Here is her own account of it:

It was early in 1914, when I was six years old. We lived on Spike Island—my father, though an Irishman from County Tipperary, being then in the British Army. We were there a number of years and a happy family we were, my father, my mother, my two elder brothers, and myself. We children played and wandered about the place and always had friendly smiles and welcomes from the people round about. My father was very psychic—uncomfortably so for him. He hated being psychic and never cultivated the gift in any way. He considered it a dangerous thing to tamper with and would be considerably upset when he saw me, from an early age, take to telling fortunes.

No one ever *taught* me to tell fortunes, and I now very much dislike telling them. I originally did so as a spur to make a party go, but I found as time went on that many times I hit the nail on the head, even telling my "victims" things due to happen in the future that I could not have known about. They strongly and emphatically regarded my prophecies as being beyond the reach of possibility and ended up, in most cases, by accusing me of not trying. So frequently did my prognostications come to pass that I could not put them down to lucky coincidence.

I mention this only by way of explanation of how I inherited from my father some small psychic gift.

The experience I am about to relate was undoubtedly a psychic experience. Even to this day the whole picture is so vivid in my memory I could paint a picture of it.

Also, I am prepared to swear that before I saw this apparition I had heard no stories about the place in question; I therefore was not "primed," and even if I had been, a beautiful, sunny summer midday would not be conducive to morbid imaginings.

My father taught me lessons himself, and every day at 12:00 o'clock it was my little task to go down to the launch that came over from Cobh on the mainland at midday to fetch his paper and get the benefit of a walk in the fresh air.

The house we lived in was about half a mile from the pier, standing only a few yards from the sea. The road I walked along skirted the sea, and as I left our house the sea would be on my right and the hill of the island on my left.

First I would pass the little chapel, then a whitewashed cottage in which lived Mrs. Reilly, who did our washing for us. Next to her cottage, but farther back, were some big red-brick military buildings, and next to that was the doctor's house.

The doctor's house would not be more than 150 yards from ours, and the path to the pier ran between it and the sea. It stood in a grove of very old gnarled trees—I always remember calling them "Arthur Rackham trees," so like they were to his drawings in my fairy-tale books of sinister-looking trees that seemed to have eyes and noses and features.

The house and garden were surrounded by a wall which fronted the road—about five feet high, I would say—and I would be due to pass right under it and could touch it with my hand as I went along.

The day I had this experience was a beautiful sunny day in late May or early June—I remember this well, because the fields were carpeted with glossy buttercups. When I left the house my mind was full of something my father had just taught me—that when the sun was at its meridian your shadow was directly under you—and as I walked the first twenty or thirty yards from the house, I was jumping around trying to get the better of the sun.

Only to find, of course, that what my father had said was true.

Absorbed in this pastime, with my eyes mostly on the ground, I happened to look up when I was about five yards away from the corner of the doctor's wall. *Something* was looking over the wall across to Cobh. I walked a few more steps nearer before I realized what it was, and then I became rooted to the ground with fear. It was not ten paces away and I could see it only too clearly.

It must have been a very tall thing that was looking over the wall, because I could almost see to its waist—and the wall was at least five feet high. It was in the *rough* shape of a human being—that is, it had a head and shoulders and arms—though I did not see the hands, which were behind the wall.

Except for two dark caverns which represented its eyes, the whole thing was of one color, a sort of glistening yellow. The only thing like it is the glistening luminosity of rancid butter that has been left in the sun.

As the wall was parallel to the road and on my left, the thing was looking past me—across the little road and straight across to Cobh.

I cannot tell how long I stood in motionless fear, gazing at this thing, but eventually *it began to turn its head very very slowly towards me!*

Petrified as I was, I heard a voice in my ear—"If it looks straight at you, Eileen, you will *die*."

My feet seemed to be anchored to the ground by heavy weights, but somehow I managed to turn and run. I ran into Mrs. Reilly's cottage about fifteen yards away.

The next thing I know was that Mrs. Reilly had my head in her lap and was sponging my face with water. I was shaking all over with shock and terror. "Oh, Mrs.

Reilly," I cried, "I saw something *dreadful* in the doctor's garden!"

Mrs. Reilly stroked my hair. "You're not the first, nor you won't be the *last* to see *that*, Alannah!"

I am glad to say I never saw it again; but I learned long after that it was common knowledge that the doctor's garden was haunted, not only by the thing I saw, which must have been an elemental, but by the ghost of an old man who had murdered his young wife.

A few years ago I got permission to visit the island— but before I go on I must say that, in spite of this experience, my two brothers, who are both now dead, and I always looked on our years on the island as the happiest years of our lives.

As I have said, I got official permission (this is now necessary) to go over the island, and was shown around by a very charming young lieutenant in the Irish Army. We went up to the fort, saw the old moat in which my parents used to play tennis, visited the sad little convicts' graveyard with its pathetic, nameless green mounds, and during our tour we passed the doctor's house.

"You won't believe me, Lieutenant Fitzgerald," I said, "but that," touching the wall, "is where I saw a ghost."

I expected a satirical, though good-mannered, response, but he answered quite seriously: "I am not surprised, for there is another ghost up at the fort. I saw it myself."

It seems that just before my visit a sentry fired a shot at the gate of the fort and was hauled over the coals for creating an alarm. He insisted that he saw a man dressed in British Army uniform emerge from a large block of buildings on the right. It was not so much the British Army uniform that caused him to shoot—it was a feeling of terror, unearthly terror.

Certainly, the man was in a desperate state; so, next night, our lieutenant stayed on duty with the sentry. The same thing happened—the same figure emerged, and Lieutenant Fitzgerald shot at it, but it walked straight on towards them, though, if it had been human, it must have been killed, and it vanished a few yards in front of them.

Next night—whether this is relevant or not, I don't know—that whole building was gutted by a mysterious fire. The figure has not been seen again.

CHAPTER X

Biddy Early

And having gotten the silver you healed that horse by
  praying to your Walliman. And there is none that
Gives you alms but they will thrive.
      Indictment of Jonet Randall for Witchcraft, 1627

Biddy Early, the great nine-
teenth century "wise woman" of County Clare, was one
of the most challenging personalities in Western Ireland
in recent times. Even today, some eighty years after her
death, she and her deeds have become a legend which
is still alive and vigorous throughout the province of
Connacht.

Often on a winter's evening in many a western cottage,
when a neighbor or two has dropped in for a pipe and a
friendly chat, the family gathers round the open hearth
and more turf is piled upon the fire till it glows again with
generous warmth. Then surely and bravely the bright

flames throw out defiance at the Atlantic gale roaring through the trees outside, and the pleasant aromatic smell of the turf will draw all nearer still, chairs will be pulled up, and steaming hot cups of tea be passed around. And while the three-legged skillet, brimful of floury potatoes, bubbles and steams cheerily as it swings from the crane just clear of the flames, men relax and talk goes easily from mouth to mouth, as smoothly as the tea cups pass from hand to hand to be refilled.

Soon the older men—and women, too—will talk of the past, of their childhood and lusty youth, and of the old tales they then heard, tales telling of older days still. Then, if the name of Biddy Early be mentioned, there will be a sudden hush. Some will glance uneasily toward the door, children will nestle closer to their mothers, and perhaps a quietly whispered "The Lord save us" will drift to the ear as softly as the plash of the gray turf ash falling upon the hearth.

But after a moment's pause the talk will begin again, for more must be told of her, and all wait in tense expectation. So, little by little, the tales unfold. Maybe an old man will take his pipe from his mouth, blow a cloud of blue smoke up to the darkness of the thatch above him, and begin, "I mind well the time, and I just a gossoon, when an old man, Michael O'Brien he was, came up here from O'Callaghan's Mills in County Clare, not far from Biddy Early in Feakle. He was a cobbler and worked round the countryside here for three or four months; mending harness mostly he was. He knew her well and thought well of her too, and would hear no hard word against her. He had a powerful way with him, so he had. He had many queer tales to tell of her, of things he had seen himself, no less." And then the stories will come and be discussed and

digested till someone else meets them with others equally
vibrant with interest.

And thus her legend survives, a real and vital thing in
western folklore and tradition. W. B. Yeats himself was
deeply interested in her and at one time contemplated
collecting her stories into a book. Sometimes in the course
of conversation he would refer to her, his resonant voice
richly intoning her name till she seemed a vibrant reality,
alive and potent still.

In his later years I was a frequent visitor to Rivers-
dale, Yeats's pleasant house in Rathfarnham, an outer
suburb of Dublin that was almost country, for he and I
had become close friends and I was deeply attached to
him. I remember well how, in the early evening of a
lovely summer's day in 1937, we were alone together as
we often were, sitting in his library. The windows were
wide open, letting in all the fragrance of the well-kept
garden. We talked of the ways of life in Western Ireland
and how old customs were still kept alive there, and we
were comparing them with things which I had met with
in my travels in India and the nearer East, when I
mentioned a specific incident about a cure that seemed
quite magical. Raising his hand with the rather dramatic
action that he often used, he stopped me to say that he
had heard the same thing almost in every detail done by
Biddy Early, "the wisest of wise women," as he then called
her, and he went on to speak of her in terms of warm
approval. Although I had often heard stories of her since I
was a child, I must confess that I had taken little interest
in her, and I bitterly regret now that I do not remember
better all that Yeats said of her on that occasion. Although
I heard him refer to her quite often both before and since,
he did so that evening more fully and intimately than at

any other time. However, it was the recollection of this talk that finally stimulated my interest in her.

It is not easy to give fair and due justice to Biddy's life, for she was a very controversial figure, and as so often happens in such cases, her powerful and highly organized enemies have done their best to blacken and belittle her reputation. Fortunately for truthful history, they have failed to do so since her death as signally as they failed during her long life.

This account of her has been compiled from a number of sources. Three old, old inhabitants of her village who knew her personally have been enlisted, as well as several of her great-granddaughters—charming and well-educated ladies now working in Dublin. A very self-contradictory attack upon her published in 1879, six years after her death, has been taken into account, as well as the general local tradition in the West. But the best source of information has been the stories of old people who in their youth had heard firsthand accounts of her from her contemporaries and personal friends. These radiate authenticity with every word and corroborate each other astonishingly, from place to place and from county to county.

Biddy Early was born in the closing years of the eighteenth century in the little hamlet of Feakle in East Clare. There she passed her life, a life that was the very opposite of uneventful till she was called to her ancestors in 1873. In her youth she was a fine, strapping, healthy country girl, well versed in all the doings and duties of country life. She could milk and churn, cook on an open turf fire, tend poultry, or smell in the air any coming rain or change of weather. All these things she could do as well as anyone else round about her, or better. She was in character strong and courageous, though rather impulsive, and was endowed with unusually quick native intelligence, which was reinforced by a very keen observation.

Though Irish was her language, she learned some English as a young woman after her first marriage. During the latter part of her life she could converse quite freely in the language of the Gall, as English was then called. From her early childhood she showed clearly that she was fey to a remarkable degree. She talked of seeing, and even of playing with, elemental beings with the same casual assurance that any other child would have in speaking of playing with a puppy or a kitten. As she grew up and began to realize more fully the doubts which more orthodox humans had of anyone who was too intimate with the inhabitants of the unseen fairy world—though they all accepted them as an obvious fact, and many claimed to have seen them on occasion—she kept herself more aloof from them, or more probably kept her psychic life and adventures more discreetly to herself.

Quite early in life, she acquired a knowledge of wild herbs and of their medicinal and other more occult properties from the earth folk, who taught her how to use them for magical and semi-magical purposes. At first she did this in a small way, protecting and, when occasion arose, curing her own family and their petty livestock. Almost imperceptibly she began to do the same good offices for her friends and neighbors as well as for their animals, provided that she happened to think well enough of them at the time, for she made a habit of being very particular about whom she would help.

Her reputation as a healer or "white" witch spread steadily, and more and more neighbors came to her with their troubles. Next, came men and women from the surrounding parishes, followed eventually by people from most of the counties of Western Ireland.

Long before her fame had reached this far, however, the war between her and the Church which lasted all her life till its closing days had broken out, for when word of her powers had begun to spread, the local parish priest intervened indignantly. Biddy had become a source of grave offense to him and a disturbing element in the smoothly running life of his parish, where hitherto his authority had been unchallenged. He was outraged to find that his authority was now ignored and actually flouted, to the scandal of his flock, by this illiterate peasant woman with her uncanny occult powers. Her powers were ungodly, he proclaimed to all and sundry.

Biddy had always been lax in her observance of the duties demanded by the Catholic Church, and its authority and dignity had carried little weight with her, even from youth. She had also, however, a very domestic side to her character, and she was married three times, always in church with a proper ceremony. Her first marriage took place in her middle twenties, her husband being a local laborer, by whom she had two sons and a daughter. But at that time her fame had not spread much beyond her immediate neighborhood. Shortly after the death of this husband some ten years later, she married again, but within another five or six years was again widowed. In due course she married her third and last husband, whom she also outlived. Her second and third marriages were childless.

By the time of her second marriage her reputation as a wise woman and as a healer was widespread, but it was not till a number of years later, after her third marriage, that she really let herself go as a full witch. She defied

the Church and all its powers, and against it she cou-
rageously and quite successfully pitted her own personal
powers: powers which were backed by the mysterious—
to many the awful and wicked—might of the unseen
elemental world. She had on her side very practical and
effective weapons which enabled her to hold her own till
she saw the final approach of death.

These weapons were the undoubted cures which she
effected, for while she could and did cure people and
animals, as well as crops, the parish priest could not; nor
could the bishop or any other member of the Irish hierarchy. Clearly, this was the acid test. When people
urgently wanted themselves or their dear ones or their
animals to be saved, it was to Biddy they turned, knowing that she alone could do so if she wished. Nothing
that the parish priest might say or do could prevent them
from going to her, even if only clandestinely, in the total
absence of any alternative cure by the Church.

The story of her cures, of her foretellings, and of
how her occult powers developed is a curious one. It may
be conveniently divided into two distinct periods, the first
of which covered her life before the advent of the famous
blue bottle. The second period spans the time from its
coming into her possession until her death in 1873.

The earlier part of her life followed in most ways the
normal course of the lives of the "wise women," who are
still fairly common. During this first period she used the
herbal and other lore which she had learned from the
earth folk, but also a spirit-given healing touch lay within
her magnetic fingers when she chose to use it. And, of
course, like all countrywomen of those days, she had the
lore and practice in these things which had been handed
down from generation to generation in her family. Country

traditions vary a great deal, according to custom and kin-
ship, and it is always difficult to find a satisfactory dividing
line between them and full-blooded magic, for each merges
into the other imperceptibly. Biddy had the skill and intelligence to use traditional lore very effectively, so that
it reinforced her occult powers until her reputation became unique.

As is the custom with most practitioners of magic
healing, Biddy Early accepted no payment. Throughout
the world and in most ages this rule in regard to magic
cures is invariable. If payment is made, the healing soon
becomes a professional and money-making matter on the
low level of the quacks and charlatans who abound. The
cures soon cease to be effective, and the healer loses his
or her real power and becomes nothing more than a quack
himself.

Because Biddy maintained this tradition strictly, she
never rose from her life of comparative poverty. She
gladly welcomed gifts, however, and as she never suffered
from undue diffidence, she let it be known what kind of
gift she expected, in the clearest way and with no beating about the bush. She had a soft palate for alcohol and, if
not by her direction at least by her happy acquiescence, her
gifts, though chiefly groceries and food, too often con-
sisted of low-grade whiskey or of the native illicit dis-
tillation, poteen.

But she unquestionably did great good with her herbal
remedies, and she took great trouble and care in making
up her preparations. She gathered her herbs herself, and
no one knew precisely how they were used. She knew
where to look for a particular wild plant, going straight
to some spot in a ditch or a wood or on an open hillside
to pluck the leaf or bud she required. Did she gather

these herbs at special hours of the day or night, or at
different seasons of the year or phases of the moon? No
one knows, but she sometimes hinted strongly that this
was so. Anyway, in due course she would produce her
concoction and give it to her client with careful instruc-
tions on how to use it.

Her life and mild adventures moved along these traditional lines until the Blue Bottle came dramatically into
her ambit and raised her activities to a tempo which could
no longer be ignored or laughed off with disbelief.

Her eldest son, at this time a lad of about nineteen,
was well known to the earth folk, though he had not his
mother's occult powers. He was a normal, healthy boy
of fine physique, with all the animal spirits and sporting
interests that a country lad should have. He was a noted
hurler, one of the best in the county, and was quite a
local hero on this account.

Late one summer afternoon the lad was coming home
from a visit to a farm some six or seven miles away and
was taking a beeline across country to his home. When
he had a mile or two to go and was striding along a
narrow country road with low-lying fields—old cut-away
bogs—on one side and a grassy bank on the other, he saw
a group of fairies standing about in one of the fields with
hurleys in their hands, obviously about to start a game.
They saw him at the same time and hailed him urgently.
It transpired that they were short of a man and asked if
he would play and make up the team. Being in a hurry,
he at first excused himself, but they pressed him so
earnestly that at last he agreed and jumped agilely down
into the field.

The match was long and vigorous, but young Early
played the game of his life, and when it ended his side

was victorious. He climbed back on to the road, anxious
to reach his home, but they delayed him a few moments
till several of them came up and presented him with a
large, empty, pale-blue bottle without a cork. The bottle
could easily be seen through. "This is the thanks we give
you," they said. "Take this back to your house and give
it to your mother."

"But what has she to do with it?" he said in astonishment. "What am I to tell her?"

"You will tell her nothing. Just give it to her. She will
know." With that they dived off the road into the bank
and disappeared into the ground in the very disconcerting
way the earth folk have.

He went straight home and without a word presented
the empty bottle to his mother. She received it in silent
astonishment too, turning it round and round in her hands
as she gazed at it with undisguised curiosity. Then she
gave a low exclamation—by no means a holy one—as she
saw the bottle gradually fill up with a kind of mist which
made it quite opaque. In a few moments she could see,
in the depths of the swirling, milky mist, figures and signs
and portents which had meaning for her.

This bottle was to be her talisman. When in doubt
about a client she looked into it. If it remained unchanged,
an ordinary, transparent blue-glass bottle, she was to send
the applicants away and refuse to help them. If, however,
it clouded up she was free to set to work to help them if
she could. But when, being anxious to help, she knew that
her own powers would not be sufficient to meet the case,
she would gaze fixedly into the cloudy depths of the bottle
until she saw there the directions she required.

Both with and without the aid of the blue bottle
she had an uncanny power of telling the future. Many

visitors were thoroughly disconcerted when, without being asked, she would announce what would happen to them in the course of the next few weeks or months, detailing petty things as clearly as those of more importance. The correctness of her foretellings was invariable.

She lived in a little cottage on a bare and windswept hill about two hundred yards north of the road from Tulla to Feakle. The small Lough Kilgarron lay about a quarter of a mile to the northeast, while the village of Feakle was nearly another mile to the east of the lough again. From the road the hill rose steeply at first and then flattened out some distance in front of Biddy's house, which was thus quite invisible from the road. The little bohereen or lane which led to her cottage from the road climbed the hill slantwise at a gentle slope, turned sharply at the top, and then ran straight to her door. The ruins of the house are to be seen today, and many a curious sightseer still makes the pilgrimage to it.

Unlike most other seers, Biddy on occasion obliged by giving racing tips, provided always that she felt so inclined and that she liked the enquirers sufficiently. Her tips are reputed to have been remarkably accurate.

The story is told that one day there was a big "flapper," or unofficial race meeting in the vicinity, just the other side of the hill from her cottage and not more than three miles away as the crow flies. A stranger from a neighboring county was bringing two horses which he intended to run in the same race. He had heard much of Biddy and of her power of foretelling the future and picking winners on the race track, but he laughed at it all as nonsense. As he rode along the high road past her home with some friends on his way to the meeting, it suddenly came into his head to test her so-called prophetic powers and catch her out. Without further ado he put his resolution into action and, so as to give her no possible clue as to what was afoot, he dismounted and walked quickly up the bohereen with two of his friends. Having knocked and been promptly told to come in, the three men entered the mud-floored cottage living room. Biddy, who was sitting on a home-made wooden chair on the far side of the open hearth, looked up at them enquiringly.

"God be with the house," said the man, using the traditional Irish greeting on entering a strange house.

Without bothering to reply in the accepted way, Biddy cut him short and came to the point with that disconcerting abruptness which she so often adopted. "So you want to know what horse will win," she said, mentioning the race the two horses were entered in. "You think the chestnut will win," she continued, "but you are wrong. The bay will win, and win well."

This certainly took him aback as, except for his formal Irish salutation, he had not opened his mouth since entering the cottage nor had the others. Yet Biddy had known what he came for, had answered his unspoken question at once, and had done so without any beating about the bush or with any attempt to cross-examine information out of him by cleverly directed questions.

She had not seen, she could not possibly have seen, the horses; they had been left quite out of sight upon the road; even less could she have known which horses were to run in which race. Altogether it was a remarkable demonstration of her powers. Still the man was not too impressed, for he knew well—or, as it turned out, he merely thought he knew—that her estimate was entirely wrong. He would soon expose her, he thought, as a bogus prophetess, for quite clearly the chestnut was by far the better horse of the two.

That night he went home a wiser though a much poorer man. He had heavily backed the chestnut but it never had its heart in the race; the bay won easily, to the delight of the local people who had supported it and to the double discomfiture of its owner.

A few years after this the parish priest decided to intervene personally and put a stop to Biddy's occult practices once and for all. He had brought all the pressure to bear upon her that he could from a distance, denouncing her from the pulpit, forbidding his flock to go near her, and even getting his bishop to denounce her too. But it was all to no purpose, for she continued serenely in her ways.

For the most part she did good, helping those in trouble far and near. However, it must be admitted that now and again she struck shrewd and telling blows of magic power—though rarely, if ever, mortally—at her enemies, especially at those who had come to her for help and later meanly turned against her to curry favor with her powerful opponents. Nor was Biddy by any means mealy-mouthed; she could, and often did, swear and abuse as potently and viciously as anyone, especially when she "had some drink taken."

So one fine afternoon the parish priest mounted his horse and rode out to her cottage, his breast swelling with righteous indignation as he went. He dismounted, tied his horse to a convenient post, and walked angrily up the bohereen to the cottage. Hardly waiting to knock, he

went in and found Biddy on her usual chair by the hearth
and neither surprised nor perturbed by his arrival. She
welcomed him in Irish with formal courtesy, but this only
served to incense the worthy father still more.

"You will not be so pleased to see me, Bridget Early,
by the time you have heard all I have to say to you," he
snapped at her. Then he settled down to tell her in no uncertain terms exactly what he thought of her, of her
behavior, and of the spirits with whom she professed to
deal. Finally he drew a vivid picture of what would
happen to her in this world as well as in the world to come
if she did not quickly mend her ways.

Biddy listened with some composure at first, if not
with amusement, but after a time she began to interrupt
him and eventually to talk back at him as vigorously as he
spoke to her. At last he was forced to stop by sheer want
of breath, so, hurling a final threat at her head as he left,
he stamped out and strode down the lane to his horse,
her parting words ringing in his angry ears. She had had
the impertinence to warn him to be careful how he went
home. He soon found out that this warning was not an
empty one at all, for his quiet old hack was in a most
restive mood and he had great difficulty in mounting it.
Having at last done so, he found that his troubles had only
begun, for she refused to move. The good father's temper,
which had become badly frayed during his interview
with Biddy, now gave way completely in the face of this
unaccountable obstinacy on the part of his favorite mount.
He beat the poor animal soundly, but the more he beat it
the more stubbornly it refused to advance a step, behaving
as if there were some invisible barrier before it which it
could not surmount.

Eventually, in desperation at the repeated blows, it reared up so high that it fell over backwards, throwing its rider heavily on to the road. Bruised and shaken, he regained his feet and walked over to the little horse, which now stood quietly in the same place, but trembling and sweating from its experiences. He took its reins and patted and soothed it for a few moments, then tried to lead it forward gently as he walked beside it; but again he failed, for the animal refused to take even one step ahead. At length, he was forced to give up the hopeless struggle and, baffled and humiliated, return to Biddy and ask her to free his horse.

As to Biddy, as soon as she saw his disheveled and dusty condition, she was filled with sincere concern. She admitted that she had prevented the horse from moving, but assured him that she had had no intention of having him thrown or of hurting his body in any way. Apologizing profoundly, she told him that the spell was now lifted from his horse and he could ride home without further trouble. Sure enough, when the father returned to his horse he found that Biddy had been as good as her word, and he rode home quietly and with much to think about.

When I was young I heard a version of this story, still to be found in Mayo, which had become considerably adorned, I am sure, in the course of time as it passed from parish to parish across the countryside. In this version, it was the bishop himself, no less, who drove out in state, with his impressive carriage and pair, to see Biddy and to hurl his episcopal thunderbolts at her head, only to be humbled to the dust by that doughty lady as his horses plunged and backed, upsetting his carriage into the ditch. Of course, this pleasantly dramatic story is quite absurd, for dignified Irish bishops do not go touring the country to wrestle in person with minor wrongdoers. Indeed, whenever I mentioned this story in Clare and Galway as I collected my information, it was received with complete derision—and rightly so. I mention this variation because it clearly shows how, though the outward trappings of these stories may be changed to suit local tastes, the essence of them remains inviolate.

Curiously enough, this encounter between Biddy and the parish priest sowed the seeds of a new mutual respect which was to bear fruit a few years later when Biddy saw her death approaching. She knew at once that she was in her last illness, and she sent for her old enemy, the parish priest, who came to her readily. A few days later she passed peacefully away in the bosom of the Church against which she had for so long rebelled.

But before she died, even before she sent for the priest, she ordered those around her to take her now-famous blue bottle and cast it far into the waters of Lough Kilgarron, putting those who undertook to do so under terrible penalties of the elemental world if they in any way or for any reason failed to do so properly. It was accordingly done, but as she had said nothing about getting it out again after she was dead, the spot was carefully marked. She hardly was buried before some of the more adventurous spirits set to work to retrieve the bottle, but they failed to find it. From that day to this, many attempts have been made to get it, but all have been unsuccessful. Only a year or so ago a rumor spread that it had been found, but the story turned out to be false. So the famous blue bottle still remains safe at the bottom of the little lough.

It is difficult to understand why there has been such a strong desire to get the bottle, for it could have no use or interest except as a curious relic; it had no power of itself but only functioned through the power given to Biddy Early. But such is the way of the world.